# ELIZABETH RENARD

## *Behind Bars*

### A SHOCKING CASE OF DEPRAVITY

outskirtspress
DENVER, COLORADO

The opinions expressed in this manuscript are solely the opinions of the author and do not represent the opinions or thoughts of the publisher. The author has represented and warranted full ownership and/or legal right to publish all the materials in this book.

Behind Bars
A Shocking Case of Depravity
All Rights Reserved.
Copyright © 2015 Elizabeth Renard
v2.0

Cover Photo © 2015 thinkstockphotos.com. All rights reserved - used with permission.

This book may not be reproduced, transmitted, or stored in whole or in part by any means, including graphic, electronic, or mechanical without the express written consent of the publisher except in the case of brief quotations embodied in critical articles and reviews.

Outskirts Press, Inc.
http://www.outskirtspress.com

ISBN: 978-1-4787-3533-5

Outskirts Press and the "OP" logo are trademarks belonging to Outskirts Press, Inc.

PRINTED IN THE UNITED STATES OF AMERICA

This book is dedicated to my husband and my five sons. Without all of you in my life, I wouldn't be here today; you have all shown me love and how to love. Also to my wonderful brother and sister; without their courage and determination our lives would have remained in darkness.

A "Thank You" is just not enough.

# Table of Contents

Author's Notes & Introduction .................................................. vii

Chapter 1: The Phone Call .................................................. 1

Chapter 2: Westmead .................................................. 7

Chapter 3: A Dog with a Bone .................................................. 15

Chapter 4: The Nightmare Begins .................................................. 18

Chapter 5: Party Time .................................................. 21

Chapter 6: Day Trips .................................................. 25

Chapter 7: Summer Holiday .................................................. 28

Chapter 8: Sunday School .................................................. 33

Chapter 9: Granny's House .................................................. 36

Chapter 10: Breaking the Record .................................................. 40

Chapter 11: The Silver Curlew .................................................. 46

Chapter 12: The Wendy House .................................................. 50

Chapter 13: The Move .................................................. 58

Chapter 14: Girl Guides .................................................. 67

Chapter 15: The Bar .................................................. 73

Chapter 16: Behind Bars .................................................. 76

Chapter 17: A Visit to the Doctor ................................. 82

Chapter 18: Get a Job ................................................... 91

Chapter 19: A Knock at the Door .............................. 103

Chapter 20: The Case and the Trial ........................... 117

Chapter 21: The Press ................................................ 141

Chapter 22: David ...................................................... 151

Chapter 23: The Sentencing ....................................... 160

Chapter 24: The Ripple Effect ................................... 171

Chapter 25: Survivor .................................................. 179

Chapter 26: Tom and I ............................................... 182

# Author's Notes & Introduction

My name is Elizabeth. This is a common name for an English girl. Saying that, though, I believe I was named after a racehorse that my father bet on in 1959. The horse was a winner. I was the first daughter; my two brothers David and Edward now had a sister. Two years later another sister followed, four children, quite normal in the sixties; we were just another average family—average on the surface, however.

This is my first book, a book that will try in its pages to fathom where this ordinary family went so wrong. In the pages that follow it will soon become clear that we were far from being ordinary. Mum and Dad used violence and shame to keep us under control, isolated us from friends and family lest their secrets be revealed, and used their threats often like "no one will believe you," or "I will kill you if you tell anyone what goes on in our house."

I hope by telling my story I can reach out to people like me; this is not and never should be accepted as normal. I am holding out my hand at the age of 51—yes, it has taken me many years to get this far. My brother David is my hero in all of this; without his courage and determination I would not be where I am today. The 9th of October 2009 was the turning point that changed all of our lives. I thank him from the bottom of my heart. I didn't know I had such a wonderful brother and sister. Thank God there are people like them on this earth, I owe them both so much; their actions changed my life, my children's lives, and so many people who have praised all of us for our courage and bravery in coming forward and being counted. I no longer carry the shame daily. I can now really start to live and not just to survive as I had done. People often ask me, "How did you manage to be so normal?" We are and can all be great actors; we have the face that says everything is fine and the face that very few people see. The insecurities, the inward loneliness and confusion. My sons kept me going most of the time and certainly kept me very busy. There was little time to pity myself or indulge in feeling sorry for myself; in a way I was shutting out all of the painful memories to cope as best I could. Some of my work friends say I am amazing and that I have unbelievable courage to go through all of this. I just know it wasn't courage, it was knowing I had to support my brother and sister in telling the truth, just the right thing to do. I have no regrets at doing so, and I have finally been released from my own prison. It is an amazing feeling; if I could bottle this feeling and give it to someone like me, or someone who may be on the brink of freeing themselves from their abused past or present, how fantastic that would be. My thanks also must extend to the 12 members of the jury who believed in us, and our barrister, Mr. Taylor, with his sensitivity in dealing with such a horrific case.

Thanks also to Hillery, Dee, Libby, Lin—they believed in us too. Don't be alone, don't hide the truth anymore, stand up and be counted, you are worth it. Our lives have been transformed, and yours can too. There is nothing special about me; I am just the same as you. You can do this too.

Take the first step.

I know it takes extreme courage but you can do it; there is help out there for you every step of the way, so go and get it. Change your life for the amazing better. My heart goes out to you reading this now; it's never too late.

I received this from my counselor, Dee. I didn't get to speak to her often, as working two jobs left very little time for counseling. I have included it because the words are powerful.

The best thing you can do is realize that there is nothing wrong with you and that it isn't your fault; everything around you is the crazy part. A victim lives in fear, a survivor endures, a victim is weak and powerless, paying for what was not their doing. A survivor grows strong because she knows the price is not hers to pay, the sin is not hers alone. I longed one day just to be happy, truly happy and smile a real smile, not because I have been drinking, not because I haven't slept in days, but because I am finally at peace. I have found peace and now I smile for no reason at all. As some may say, "I am on a pink cloud and I ain't letting it go." I am proud, proud of me, I fought to keep going and succeeded, I felt like giving up but never did, I kept going.

My experiences have made me more determined to fulfill my dreams and live my life to the fullest. I guess what I am trying to say is that I won and always will because there is nothing anyone can do to me that will take away who I am. I hope this reaches out to you.

Elizabeth

CHAPTER 1

# The Phone Call

**October 9, 2009**

I have just finished the boring housework tasks and taken a cup of tea and a cigarette into the conservatory. Looking in the mirror before sitting at the dining table, I see my blonde hair is now thinning and going quite white with age. Looking closely, more wrinkles seem to appear every second. Being just five feet tall, housework tasks can be such a challenge, and how much I begrudge spending my day off work doing even more work; oh well never mind, it's done now. Maybe I can relax for an hour or so until son number five is home from school. The youngest of my boys is twelve; he is quite a character. He seems to be growing every second and can eat for England; his red—no, he would be upset if I called it red—he is proud of his ginger hair.

Anyway, just got an hour or so before his stuff clutters the house and I end up falling over his shoes in the kitchen; no really, he is a great lad and I love him to bits. Sometimes he gets lonely, as his brothers don't say much to him. There are four or five years between each of them so they all have their own interests. And rarely visit, only when they want something—a lift here or "Can you lend me some money, Mum?" Why can't they stand on their own two feet? Do I have "Cash" point-tattooed on my forehead? Sometimes I wonder. As there are five boys and as you do when you want to grab their attention, I often get tongue-tied and can get their names wrong, so in order the eldest is 29, 26, 22, 18, and last but not least our youngest; I may refer to them as son number 1, 2, 3, 4, and 5 from time to time. My friends at work find this hilarious as they can relate to this easier; a sense of humor is a must when raising *five* hungry growing lads, and a full larder helps. On my fridge I had a notice to all teenagers: *Leave home while you still know it all.* I'm sure when they reach puberty they turn into aliens. Oh well, I am approaching the stage of alien number five. I have weathered the storm of four, so one more is not going to faze me. As I sipped my very hot tea, the only way I like it, my mind starts to wander. Maybe I should call my sister and see if she is at home; I really need adult company. A few weeks earlier she rang me saying something about David, but I was not really listening to her. Sarah didn't work, we were like chalk and cheese, so different. She loved her food and piled on the pounds easily; that sounds awful but she will often say so herself, and she was envious of me as I remained a size ten despite being stretched by five babies. She didn't know then that I have always hidden my eating problem from everyone else as well. I found food such a chore that I would easily go

# THE PHONE CALL

a day without. As long as my family had plenty I didn't really care about myself, constantly nagging the boys for picking and not sitting for a proper meal together; they seem to have such busy lives. In my job at the superstore I was always trying not to worry when thinking about them, telling them regularly "if I nag you it's because I care" and "sorry, it comes with the job title, I can't help it." The phone call to my sister had slipped my mind for now. I glanced around the conservatory and then looked out of the window. The world outside seemed like such a strange place to me. I go to work and clean my house, and that is about it. I read the occasional book. There must be more than this out there for me, thinking to myself I have got to get out more. My mind drifted again thinking of little Jake and Jemma, my two grandchildren. How I would love to see them more often. Things between the kids' parent and me, well, were not great, which had put a great strain on the relationship between me and my eldest.

Working the odd hours and weekends until late did not help; what I would give to be a proper granny and not have to work my socks off to survive. Spending quality time with them is like a dream; maybe one day when I retire, I keep thinking.

To say I am not a religious person is not strictly true; I do sometimes pray that I can one day stop to smell the roses and take some time for me. I started to reminisce about our move to this house after running a local news agents shop as manageress and son number three was just a few weeks old. We first occupied the flat above the shop, and even then it was a constant struggle raising the boys in a shop. Up at the crack of dawn seven days a week; looking back now I wonder how I did it. Things didn't work out and it was getting harder to make ends meet, so Tom and I had to get out of there. Also, before moving to the shop I worked in a petrol station doing night shifts whilst heavily pregnant, then a day shift in the shop. I must have looked like a zombie for three months before moving shortly after the birth. To keep myself awake at night I would eat chocolate and crisp; this helped the baby to pile on the weight, and for me he was a large baby. Why did I have to do it all? I kept thinking. Although married, my marriage was a complete farce. I was breadwinner wife and mother and tired of all of this. Our relationship was very rocky; yes my husband worked, but from the word go he never supported me and the boys financially.

From the age of seven, work was no stranger to me. I had to earn money for food and clothes by occupying several paper rounds, and babysitting was included for the manager of the paper shop. It became obvious to me that no one was going to provide for me and that I had to look after myself; this was my life, and married or not I had to accept it.

Tom liked drinking more than his boys or me; it became his life so we were strangers under the same roof.

Jolted from all of my thoughts, the telephone started ringing; it made me jump and as I got up to answer the call, I knocked over the last sips of my tea. Oh blow it. "Hello, is that Elizabeth?"

# THE PHONE CALL

Wondering who I was speaking to. Cautiously I answered, "Speaking." "This is PC Miles from Avon & Somerset Police." I was taken by surprise as I couldn't imagine what the police would want with me. Anxiously I answered again, "Yes, speaking." PC Miles continued, "Your brother has reported allegations of abuse by your father, do you think these allegations could be true?" My heart sank to the floor; I couldn't speak for what seemed like ages. The whole of my childhood years flashed before my eyes. This is what my sister tried to tell me; oh why didn't I listen to her? "Hello? Hello?" the voice on the phone had continued as if we had been cut off or I had disconnected the call. "Are you okay?" Stuttering with shock I answered "yes," then I said, "I think you need to come and see me." "OK," she said, "then can I come and see you this afternoon?"

"I am alone until 4:15, so that would be okay," I replied. "Can I have your post code, as I don't think I have ever been to your town," she said. I knew that from where she was it would take about forty-five minutes to get here, or in traffic would take about an hour. As I put the phone down, my mind was working overtime. David and me, well we had grown apart and hadn't spoken or had any contact for over 22 years. Remembering I had a notepad in the sideboard drawer, I pulled it out. Nobody knew about my personal notes, that for the last few years I had written things in it, very personal things about my childhood. I had read in one of the books that writing down bad things that happen can help to deal with things. Like self-counseling, it was my way of coping with the past. The next hour seemed like a lifetime. Pacing up and down with my stomach doing somersaults, things kept popping into my head; now my head is full of flashbacks, painful flashbacks. I tried so hard to shut them out, but there they were in my head in full colour, my childhood of horrors now running riot in my head. Where do I begin? I thought as I started literally chain-smoking. Not only are all these terrible memories attacking me, but the realization of what could happen was mapped out in my brain already. I visualized going to court, giving evidence—all of it. The memories still flooding my head like a broken dyke, holding all of this back for 40 years and suddenly collapsing; the more I tried to shut out all of the hurt, the more it bombarded me. Then I thought of Sarah, I must ring her now. Picking up the phone I dialed her number. "Hi—" Before I could say another word, she told me the police were coming to see her too. I promised to ring her after the police had left my house; she said "OK" and put the phone down. I could tell that she had been crying.

CHAPTER **2**

# Westmead

Born in a small two-bedroom flat, at 10 days old we moved to Westmead. Dad and Mum's first house, and I suppose the perfect place to raise two small boys and a new baby. As I grew and my little sister came along, we shared a room and the boys shared theirs. The house was sparse; there wasn't much in the way of furniture or heating—the open coal fire in the grate was about as warm as it got. There was no heating upstairs, making it bitterly cold in the winter, and also there was an infestation of mice. At night we would try to sleep, but the bitter cold and continual scratching and squeaking of mice made sure we stayed wide awake, one blanket each, and as the mice ran across the blanket we would hold our breaths as the sounds continued, scratching and squeaking all night long and our warm breaths filling the cold room. The floor was cold to stand on; lino in those days was cheap and cheerful. We girls had to take a bucket to bed with us, as we had a downstairs toilet outside the back door; on one side was the coal house and the other the toilet. Quite often

### BEHIND BARS

the water in the loo would freeze. The boys took their bucket to bed as well just in case they needed a wee in the night. Dared we complain about any of this, we would surely get a severe beating. Watching my mother on several occasions beat my brothers almost senseless put the fear of God into me. Mother was a small woman with black tied-back hair that was kept in a bun. I would look at her eyes in her moments of temper; they were dark eyes, full of evil is the only way I could describe them. Severe beatings were a daily occurrence as she made herself angry over the slightest thing. One by one we all bore the brunt of her anger, and when Dad came home we would receive even more from him. He was a short man with swept-back receding blond hair, his one good eye capable of sending shivers through any child's spine. His glass eye fixed in a permanently open state earned him the name (as we kids called him) "the one-eyed monster." There was never a kind word from Mum and Dad, never "I love you," never a cuddle or mummy kiss. From a very young age we walked around the house like walking on eggshells. My mother's mood was so fragile that the slightest thing would set her off, then she would lash out and the beatings would start; there was no escape anywhere that was safe from her anger towards us. I was kept home from school often until the cuts and bruises had subsided or faded enough so she could blame me for being clumsy—"oh a trip or fall down the stairs"; the teachers believed all her stories, no questions were ever asked.

Mealtimes, or any food for that matter, were infrequent; often no electricity or gas and winters so bitterly cold; my mother was a lousy cook at the best of times. Sunday lunches consisted of almost raw chicken blood still seeping from the carcass, raw-ish white cabbage and boiled potatoes—well sort of boiled. The gravy consisted of an Oxo cube crumbled in a cup with boiled water poured into it. We never once ate around a table or talked about normal things; in fact, we rarely spoke as we knew this would trigger her anger once again. One meal on a Sunday was it. We dared not eat it or breathe a word, so we ate in silence. Mum would stand over us with a slice of dry bread; it was disgusting to watch her fold the bread into a quarter of its size, dip into a cup of Oxo, then shove the whole thing into her mouth whilst cursing at us. Bread and spit spilling out as she ate and talked; "you better eat all of that or else," she would say and cuss.

She had gained quite a few pounds since having us children, and for her height was overweight. Dad was the opposite, skinny; he was never given the same food as we had to endure, and I rarely saw him eat anything other than sandwiches. In the spring, the Sunday afternoon chore was weeding the garden. This consisted of two long strips of earth; the boys would do one side, and we girls the other. Playtimes did not exist. I don't think they had any maternal instincts for us and just used us for chores, cleaning the house, washing and gardening, etc. Very little praise or recognition ever came our way. My brother Edward was around ten years old, David eight, me seven, and Sarah five. We so wanted to be just normal kids

◄ BEHIND BARS

and run around and play, but the only time we were able to do that was at school. All four of us were there at the same time with my sister just starting. In between the nasty taunts about the way we dressed and bullying, we would get time to run around and play. Next door to Longacre Road School was a senior school for boys. The two schools were separated by a steel fence. As my brothers grew and went to senior boys school, I would often see them running around their playground; it was good to know that Mum and Dad couldn't stop us from doing this. Sometimes Mum would send us out of the house come rain or shine and tell us not to come back until the end of the day; from our house we would walk for miles through the fields towards Filton (this was about the time Concord was to make its first flight). With a pocket full of picked gooseberries and blackberries, we would make our way to the Filton aerodrome and listen to her engines roaring. I was amazed when I saw this beautiful shape in the sky as she made her first takeoff. I dreamed one day of taking a trip on Concord; I lay in the grass with the sun beating down and closed my eyes. One day, I thought, one day. Only dozing for what seemed like a few seconds and waking with a start: I had just been stung by a wasp on my arm—my scalded arm; although the scald was old and had happened last year, it was still healing—and now it began to swell. Oh no! If she sees this I will be called stupid; Mum loved calling me stupid and useless, and at the age of seven, I believed her. When my arm got scalded with boiling water, the skin from my shoulder to my wrist blistered and peeled. Mum covered it with Vaseline, and as she rubbed in the jelly I screamed so loud as the skin continued to fall off. I didn't understand why she was so angry with me, as I did nothing wrong, but hey, I had begun to learn that this was normal for my mother. My scars are still visible today and don't really bother me, but in the summer people ask me, "whatever happened to your arm?" I never told anyone what happened years ago, but now that I am free from all my past, I can tell.

After surviving on wild fruit all day it was beginning to get dark, so I made my way home with David; he was still so excited about Concord and went on about how amazing it was. Feeling very tired and hungry we finally made it home, both of us dreading what sort of mood we would be greeted with. When we arrived home with very sore feet there was no one there; the house was in darkness. Mum had disappeared. I tried to get in but all the windows and doors were firmly shut. We sat outside on the curb and waited for what seemed like hours. It must have been about 9:30 pm when I looked down the road and caught sight of Mum; she didn't look happy about something and my brother was holding his arm. As they approached Mum yelled at us; poor little Sarah was lagging behind her. "Where have you been? Get in the house before I beat the living daylights out of you." Her ranting continued. "He's broken his arm," she snapped. "Stupid git." He had been playing and slipped off a small wall that ran around the local hospital. Although Edward had given the nurse his name and address, Mother did not go straight to the hospital in a state of panic, but told the nurses, "Oh well he is in the right place, I will collect him later when you have set his arm." As we finally got into the house, we were ordered straight to bed. As I lay in my bed, my tummy was rumbling so loudly from hunger. I could see David in the other room too. Sarah was sent up to bed shortly after me, and her belly was rumbling louder than mine. "Have you had anything to eat?" I asked her. "No," she said. We never referred to meals as being breakfast, dinner, or tea, as these were totally strange to us. She blurted out that Edward had to stay up until Dad came home, even though he had already had a slap from Mum. She was adamant that he deserved another from Dad. I could hear him crying. Even at my tender age at seven, I was very depressed and desperate to escape this hell called home. I tried to sleep but my arm was still throbbing and hurting from the wasp sting. I slowly rocked my head back and forth, chanting my times tables. This used to drive my sister crazy, but today she thanks me because she learned them off by heart. Sound asleep I'm dreaming I must be, I'm falling, falling—*bang*, I hit the floor. A voice yells, "Get out of bed! I want the bedding!" It was barely light outside and my sore arm hit the floor first. I turned to Sarah in a daze, having been woken so abruptly. Mum was tearing the sheets out from under me whilst I was still asleep; maybe she thought I would remain in bed like yanking a tablecloth off a table and leaving everything standing. As I looked across to Sarah, Mum did the same to her, tearing the bedclothes from her bed. The cold lino floor sent her down with a thud; in shock we both pulled our remaining blanket around us and she started to cry. I tried to keep her quiet as I knew that her crying would only aggravate Mum more. "Please don't, you will get a slap, stop crying." As I told her this, I could hear the boys, one thud after another as they both also hit the floor. I didn't understand what was going on, why did she hate us so much? What had any of us done that was so bad? I desperately needed to feel loved and wanted as a child, but there was nothing but contempt, and in those piercing dark eyes, hatred for her own children.

Over the next few weeks, the household chores intensified as David and I were punished for staying out. Edward was unable to do his share and Sarah was a little bit too young. We didn't have a washing machine or a spin dryer, so all the laundry was done in the bathtub. This was quite heavy work for a seven-year-old, but I didn't dare complain. I would rub the washing with my hands, then run the cold tap to rinse off the Omo (Mum always used Omo soap powder). Then I dragged it downstairs in a tin bucket and out into the garden to the mangle. Many times I caught my fingers in the rollers. The good old mangle, having stood outside in all weathers, was on its last legs and rusting away. As I threaded the first of the sheets through and turned the handle, it snapped off. Holding the broken piece in my hand, my heart stopped: I knew I would get a beating for this. Sure enough, Mum had spotted me from the kitchen window, and out she came at me like a mad gorilla. I was dragged upstairs and thrown into my bedroom; I hit the cold floor, again landing on my bad arm. "You will get a hiding when your father comes home, you stupid little cow." She slammed the door and stomped off back downstairs. This now meant she had to put the washing on the line very wet; how inconvenient for her. When Dad got home she told him that I had been swinging on the handle; I wasn't doing any such thing—again another one of her stories to ensure I would get a beating. I heard him marching upstairs toward my room. I held my breath, and knew, here it comes. As Dad flung open the door, he grabbed me and started shaking me. Grabbing my bad arm and squeezing it very tightly—the pain was unbearable. He slapped me across my face and I fell backwards onto my bed. I was trying so hard not to cry but failing; the more I cried the more I was slapped—slapped until I no longer felt any pain and passed out. When I came around I was alone in my room and my tummy was talking: no food again. The door opened and Sarah came to bed.

She looked at me and taunted, "You broke the mangle, it's your fault." She climbed into bed and turned away from me. My lip was fat, and the blood on the pillow told me my bottom lip had been split. I could now feel every bruise and my body ached. Slipping out of my clothes, I got back into bed. I was so hungry, but asking for food would be my last request. Covering up with my one itchy blanket, I dozed off. During the night, I heard someone hammering on the front door; this was directly under our bedroom window. *BANG BANG!* Dad went down to see what all the fuss was about. "It's the police!" a voice shouted.

CHAPTER 3

# A Dog with a Bone

"Open the door," a voice demanded. "What the hell is going on?" Dad yelled. Mum got up and stormed down the stairs. "Do you mind if we come in?" The two police officers stood in the doorway. "We have found something in the street that is very disturbing, we are not only talking to you but all of your neighbours as well." I crept out of bed to the top of the stairs, trying to listen. Sarah seemed to sleep through all of this, and the boys peeped around the door of their bedroom. "What's going on?" I put my finger to my mouth and said "shhh!"

We all listened as the two policemen talked. Mum was furious at being disturbed in the early hours and complained until she was told to shut her big fat gob. These words made me chuckle, and as I did my lip stung and I winced with pain. The voices became muffled as I struggled to hear. Then Mum came back up the stairs, and I darted back into bed. I could hear her rummaging in her bedroom. She took a wad of paper back down the stairs and the talking continued. All I could make out was that it was something to do with a dog. Everyone seemed to have dogs then, although we didn't. The dogs roamed the streets without a care and the owners allowed it. Sometimes they would form little packs of three or four. This was not unusual in Westmead, as there were no dog wardens or dog patrols as there are today. Pavements were fouled and children still played in the streets, often going home with dog mess on their clothes and shoes; barking dogs were the norm day and night. Thank God things have changed and it is no longer acceptable for a dog to roam free and terrorize children. Our neighbour's dog had bitten me on more than one occasion. Back then there was nothing you could do about it. It was not unusual to see two dogs stuck together in reproductive mode and neighbours trying to separate them with sticks or buckets of water, or anything they could lay their hands on. Dad yelled up the stairs, "I want you all to come down here now." That demanding voice that we dared not defy. I woke Sarah. "Get up! We have to go downstairs." She was dazed and confused and pushed me away. "Leave me alone," she said. "Get up, Dad said we have to go downstairs." The word "Dad" soon made her shift. I grabbed her hand and headed towards the stairs; the boys were already in the front room. Mum grabbed both of them and made them stand by her. As we entered she put on a wry smile and a pretend happy voice. "Come here," she said, "over here and stand by your brothers." One of the policemen didn't have a uniform on. I looked at him and he had a kind face, and as I passed him he smiled at me. For a brief moment a well of excitement went through me. Do they know that Mum and Dad are not nice to me? No, not just me but all of us. Have they come to take us to a mum and dad that cuddle and love children? A new mum and dad that don't beat children? I hope so, I really hope that is why they are here. All of these thoughts raced through my head. Sometimes at night I would put my hands together and pray, "Please, God, can I have a new mummy and daddy?" Mum pointed to the papers that the seated policeman was holding. "You see," she said, "you see, that is Edward's birth certificate and then David, Elizabeth, and Sarah. I do not have any other children, and I don't know why you think I may have had a baby recently. These are my children and that is that." I looked at the plain-clothed policeman and his smile had gone. "What happened to your lip?" he asked. Mum then snapped, "Oh kids fighting, you know how it is." My heart sank as I knew he had believed what she told him. My conscience was yelling at me, "Tell them, tell them both the truth." I knew they would be going soon and I would still be here. "Go back to bed," Mum said, her voice high pitched and soft as though she was a different person. As I got to the top of the stairs I stayed to listen; the boys went back to bed and so did Sarah. Dad kept repeating everything he was hearing from the police. "A baby, you say a baby?" He went on, "A neighbour's dog found a baby's arm and was dragging it in his mouth down the street." "What, five doors away from us?" He sounded really shocked, but Mum just continued to insist that it was not her baby. As far as I know, the rest of the baby's body was never found. All of the neighbours were quizzed but the case was never solved.

CHAPTER **4**

# The Nightmare Begins

Dad worked long hours in the summer and Mum often had a garden full of neighbours' kids. Whilst they were going to the local shops they would ask, "Can I leave them here, I won't be a tick." "Yeah," she would say. Mum would get a chair from the kitchen, then sit in the sunshine and crochet for hours on end whilst the kids would chase each other around the garden. Outside of the garden area, these same kids bullied or poked fun at us; we were despised by them most of the time, calling us names like "gypos" and "scum." We were so scruffy compared to them. All of our clothes had been passed down and patched up many times, and were not fit even for a jumble sale. Mum attempted to knit and the results gave the local kids even more to bully us about. Her mutilated odd wool jumpers made us a laughingstock. We were forced to wear what she wanted us to wear; we really did look scruffy and untidy. Constantly taunted by neighbours' kids, such as "smelly kids got loads of nits doo dah doo dah." Once one

## THE NIGHTMARE BEGINS

started the rest would join in, and the chanting would get louder and louder. Mum put her crochet down and called us all into the house. The other kids all gathered around the back door, which was wide open to a view of a very basic kitchen. As I turned around, one of the girls had her fingers pinching her nose. "This house stinks," she said. I think they had gathered around the door expecting Mum to give out sweets or biscuits or something; we didn't ever have anything like that in our house. Mum boiled some pans of water on the stove and began to fill the kitchen sink with hot water. "Right," she said, "who's first?" I turned in horror. I knew what she was about to do. "Strip off," she told me. "Dad will be home, you've got to have a wash. I was just seven, only seven years old but I did not want to strip off in front of the street kids—they already had loads to pick on me about; this would make their day. I would never be able to go to school in peace or show my face. I knew I couldn't argue with her, though; she would rip my clothes off me if I didn't do what she had said. As I lifted up my leg, I could hear them all snigger as they watched from the doorway. I felt so humiliated, ashamed, and embarrassed, so angry at my mum for making me do this in front of other kids. She didn't tell them to go and play, she just carried on oblivious to their sniggers and giggles. The chair then was put by the sink and I had to stand on it stark naked and had to be washed. I began to cry. "What are you crying for? I will give you something to cry about," she said. "Stand still," she yelled, and the kids just carried on sniggering. Those painful memories are so vivid

## BEHIND BARS

even today. The same with my brothers and sister when it was their turn; I'm sure they felt the same as I did. As I write this even now, I have had to stop as the tears begin to flow. The shame I felt then at the age of seven was just the starting block for what was to come.

CHAPTER 5

# Party Time

My Uncle Phil became a regular visitor in the evening with his wife Mary. She was Mum's sister, so Dad's brother Phil and Mum's sister got married, and then Uncle Steve lived two streets away on Greenslade Avenue. Uncle Steve's house and our house were worlds apart—very posh with carpets, nice curtains, and immaculate children. May was one of the children, Shaun was the eldest, then Molly and Sam, twins, all of them immaculate compared to us. We certainly lived below the poverty line. I now find this really strange as Uncle Steve and my dad worked together earning the same money. I do know now that money was not the problem, it was just that Mum and Dad would rather spend it on themselves than provide for us children. Dad made Mum a wooden box on wheels with a handle so that she could put her shopping in it. Not much bigger than a milk crate for her weekly shop. When shopping with her, there would be six or seven small items in her box—that was her weekly shop. A few packs of rich tea biscuits, tomato soup, a few potatoes, a white cabbage, and a small chicken. For a family of six people, it was nowhere near enough. When it was gone two days later she would not buy any more; in the middle of the week she would buy her Omo soap powder, and that was it. Dad would come home from work with big tins of Party Seven—huge tins of lager that had to be opened very carefully as the froth would spill out all over the side of the cans and sometimes spray up the wall. Their parties usually began on a Friday and by 6 o'clock we would be confined to the bedrooms. Sometimes we would have a packet of crisp; when that was the case, I thought I was in heaven. I would savour every crisp and try to make them last in my mouth as long as I could. Trying so hard not to crush them, I could make a packet of crisp last an hour. Mum would ensure she had her bottle of gin and Dad his whiskey. Mum and Dad would first start off in the local pub having a few drinks and leaving us to our own devices. My brother, just barely ten, was expected to be responsible for us all. They would roll in from the local pub quite merry. The local pub at the top of the street was a regular watering hole at the weekends for them. Staggering through the front door, they didn't give us a second thought. Mum would get the nibbles out for the party, then the next-door neighbours came and people from across the road. Along with Uncle Phil and Aunty Mary. Then the music would go on. Dad suddenly developed a taste for reggae music and he would play it quite loud. Some of the words to the song I didn't understand: "birth control," "fatty fatty," and "wet dream." The more they drank, the louder the music became with their voices shouting over the total din. It was strange to hear our neighbours Mr. and Mrs. Howarth shouting above the music and to be here so late in the evening. Mum was always telling us to be quiet because Mr. and Mrs. Howarth went to bed early as they were elderly.

Mrs. Howarth, I liked her. Sometimes I would come home from school and Mum would be out, so I would knock on the house next door. She always had a warm smile and tea and biscuits. I know I probably shouldn't have, but she always put biscuits on a plate and I would take two and put one in my pocket to save for bed. Never knowing if I was going to get anything to eat when Mum came home—more than likely not. If it wasn't for free school dinners, which I absolutely adored—all that jam, roly-poly custard, semolina pudding, school dinners were heaven to me—I would have probably starved to death.

The partying continued well into the night. Dad was also busy with his camera, taking lots of photographs that he loved to develop himself. Partying was a great excuse to get the camera out. Finally they would go quiet about 2 am and everyone went home. Sleep never came easy to me so I accepted all this disruption on weekends. Coming home from school one afternoon I was surprised to find the back door ajar; walking in I called out to Mum but there was no answer. Taking my little reading book, I went upstairs to my bedroom. When I got to the top of the stairs, I noticed Mum and Dad's bedroom door was open. This was very rare; usually it was bolted and locked with a heavy padlock. Curious to know what Mum's room looked like, I entered cautiously. As I

## BEHIND BARS

entered I saw spread out on the bed lots of home-developed photos. I picked them up to have a closer look. What was this? Pictures of my mother, my uncle, and the neighbours all doing things with no clothes on. I didn't understand. Is this how to party? I thought to myself. I had never seen a man or grown woman's bits before; I didn't know what to make of it all. Moving the photos around the bed and eyeing all of them, the faces I saw made me gasp. Mr. and Mrs. Howarth, Uncle Phil, Mary, Uncle Ray, Dad and Mum, and more people I recognized all naked and doing things to each other, Uncle Phil sticking his willy into my mother and Mother with Uncle Ray, her own brother's willy in her mouth—I couldn't stop staring at these photographs.

The door creaked downstairs. Mum's back, I thought. I dashed out of her room and back into my own. She rushed upstairs and quickly bolted and locked her bedroom door. Turning to me she said, "Have you been in there?" "No no," I lied. "You had better not or you will get the biggest hiding of your life," and with that she turned and headed back down the stairs into the front room. How could I tell anyone what I had seen in those photos, and who would believe me anyway? People would say I had a vivid imagination or that you want to watch what your dirty mouth is saying.

CHAPTER 6

# Day Trips

"We are going out," said Dad one Sunday afternoon. Yippee, no weeding today, I thought.

Sunday lunch was always challenging to eat. None of us had the nerve to complain; eating was always done in silence.

When we kids had finished the washing up, in washing powder—Omo as I recall, it was the only powder our Mum used; Omo was used for just about everything, even for washing our hair—Dad was waiting in the car. We all had to squash in the back of his Triumph Herald sports car. It was such a squeeze. Mum jumped into the passenger seat and we set off. The journey seemed to take ages. Finally we arrived at a place that had lots of rocks and steep cliff faces. "Where are we?" I asked. Mum snapped back, "Never you mind." We were allowed out of the car and told to follow Mum and Dad. Climbing a few rocks that stood out from the cliff base, Dad found a flat large area for him and Mum to sit on. Mum had a small blanket that she placed on the ground. "Go and play, you lot," said Dad. Looking around I could see cliffs and some fallen rocks.

Looking up at the rock face, I began to find a way to climb it; the boys and Sarah all followed. When I think of this now it scares me: we had no ropes or safety hats. There seemed to be just the will to climb that kept us on those rocks. In some of the crevasses, wild strawberries grew. I picked them as I climbed. Wow, they tasted so good. Never once did Mum or Dad think we might be in danger or ask us to be careful.

On reaching the top and moving away from the edge, we had a great view. We could see other climbers with all their safety gear halfway up the cliff face.

Soon it would be time to go home. The sun was beginning to go down. We carefully climbed down to where Mum and Dad were stretched out on the blanket. My eyes could not quite take in what I saw as my feet finally stood on part of the blanket. Dad had his trousers undone and Mum had no top on. She was rubbing Dad's willy and he was groaning. They didn't stop or cover themselves up and I didn't know where to look. The boys and Sarah had also witnessed this, and they too were upset by Mum and Dad's games. I tried to pretend I hadn't seen anything and wandered off to pick some wildflowers. On the way home the car was deadly silent as none of us wanted to talk. As young as we all were, we didn't understand what was happening back on that rock, but none of us were comfortable with it.

## DAY TRIPS

During the summer their trips became a regular day out, and so did their games. We would sometimes go on trips to some sort of muddy beach, where their games got even more daring. Mum would sit on Dad and move up and down. Then he would make her bend over and put his willy into her. All this would take place in view of the passenger train, which ran frequently. Again we kids would try to blot out the games they played. The games became normal for them.

Things began to happen to me as I tried to sleep.

Dad came into my room at night and put his bony fingers under my blanket. Pulling my legs apart, he would put his fingers in me. I cried so often and was so angry with both of them. The hidings from my mother and the abuse from my father. I was nearly eight years old. At eight I became withdrawn and unable to concentrate on my schoolwork. Mr. Worsly, who taught maths, pulled me out in front of the class and called me a dunce on more than one occasion.

I don't have any fond memories of school life or friends—just painful memories of bullying and torment. My last day of school was great.

CHAPTER 7

# Summer Holiday

The summer seemed to last longer in the late sixties. Weeks of glorious sunshine. Quite a red suntan I would end up with, so burned. Being so fair-skinned and blonde, even now I have to be careful in the sunshine. Only rich people had things like sun cream and sun hats. They were only for the posh.

From early morning, we went outside into the garden and had to stay outside until almost bedtime. "I want to do housework," Mum would say and then lock us out. Sometimes late in the afternoon we had a slice of bread and jam; that was considered enough for the day. We would get water from the sink in the toilet outside the back door. This was as close to the house as we could go.

David would stand on an old upturned tin bucket and peep through the window, often seeing Mum asleep on the sofa. He would have been in so much trouble if she saw him looking in. Luckily she never did. We never dared to disturb her, as the consequences would have been very painful. On the odd

## SUMMER HOLIDAY

occasion she would put us all outside the door and then give Edward a thrupenny bit (old money in pounds shillings and pence, pre-decimal coinage; 3d), he would go to the local shops and buy Rainbow Drops at 1/2d each and share them out for all of us. I still see them today and not much more expensive, considering it has been over 40 years since buying them. We would try to make them last all day. Sitting on the pavement outside the house, I would separate all the different colours and count them—anything to make them last longer.

Sometimes Dad would not come home until very late and we all had to be in bed. The boys would take their wee bucket to bed and then I had to take ours. Once in bed we were not allowed downstairs as the main door to the front room would be locked and bolted. Hence we couldn't go to the toilet so we had to wee in the bucket. The long hot summers made the wee smell so strong in our room and we also had to poo when needed; the stench was awful.

Bedtime, I dreaded. I knew if I went to sleep Dad's creepy hands and smelly breath would soon wake me up. Chanting the times tables and rocking my head backwards and forwards on the pillow would tire me and only then would I doze off.

"Dad has got a tent," said Edward out of the blue one day. "We are going on holiday."

Sure enough the following day Dad packed as much as he could into his tiny car, then made us sit on top of the camping gear all the way to the seaside. One stop for petrol was made on the way, but no time to use the toilet. Sarah wet herself and so did I. Tears streamed down her face as she whispered to me that she couldn't hold on. I tried hard also but the pain was getting so bad. Both Mum and Dad were unaware that we were sodden through. It was such a hot day and we were melting in the back of the car. Hopefully we would be dry by the time the car stopped. I was thinking of the telling off and smacks that would surely come if they suspected that we had both wet ourselves.

The boys had an idea that all was not well in the backseat, but said nothing. I was grateful for that at least. The journey seemed endless and uncomfortable; Dad hit every bump in the road. After what seemed like an eternity, the car stopped. A sign I could just make out said "The Dovecot and Fiddle – Camping and Caravans." I didn't know what a caravan was; I had never seen one and didn't know anyone lucky enough to have one. As Dad got out of the car, he put his seat forward and then opened the tiny boot to get the tent out. "You can get out now," he said. As I looked across the field I was amazed to see all the different cars and tents—all shapes, sizes, and colours. The caravans looked great too. Turning to Sarah I remarked, "I'm going to own a caravan when I grow up." She just laughed at me.

"Come here you two," Mum shouted. "What's this?" She pointed to both our dresses; the look on her face said it all. She was so angry that we had wet ourselves and she would make sure we paid for it. As she raised her voice, people in the field stared at her and tutted. She then lowered her voice but continued to chastise us. Dad was busy trying to unfold the tent and put the frame together. The boys tried to help sorting out all of the poles. The bright orange canvas was soon in place. Then all the other camping bits were unloaded and placed inside the tent. "Now we've got this up, it's time for a drink, let's go to the clubhouse, Lil." Lil was Dad's pet name for Mum. Looking back now I suppose it did suit her; as I grew this became short for "little insane lady."

Off to the clubhouse we went, where Dad had a whiskey and Mum had her gin. Sarah had to share a bottle of Coke and a packet of crisps with me and the boys had the same. The jukebox in the corner was playing "A Hard Day's Night" by The Beatles and I began to dance a little. This was fun. Grabbing Sarah's arm, we both began to dance. Then the music changed to "Twist and Shout." She giggled as we danced. At the other end of the room was a small platform, so we headed for it and danced for ages. Both Mum and Dad were too busy drinking to notice, so we slipped outside into the fresh air. The room was full of people smoking and drinking.

It was beginning to get dark outside. I noticed the boys in the field near the tent; it looked like they were kicking a ball around. "Look, Sarah, look at the white birds over there, they are beautiful." "Those white birds are doves, my lovely." A woman bent down to talk to me. "Put out your hand," she said. "Go on, take it." I gingerly put out my hand and the tall lady put some bird food on it. One of the doves landed on my hand. I was so thrilled, it was beautiful. "There you go," she said. "They won't hurt you." Sarah ran towards me and

## BEHIND BARS

scared it away. During the next few days, I would just sit and watch those beautiful birds whenever I could. It was the best bit of the holiday for me.

It was soon all over and we had to pack up and go home. We didn't go to the beach or see the sea or even feel the sand in our toes, but I loved those beautiful doves.

CHAPTER 8

# Sunday School

"Where is Edward?" I asked one Sunday as we started the usual weeding in the garden. "He's at Sunday school," David announced. "Dad don't like it, Dad don't want any of us going to Sunday school, we might like it and he has to put a stop to that. I heard Dad shouting at Edward about it yesterday."

I wondered what Sunday school was like. Was it the same as school? Why would Edward want to go if it was? At school it was horrible, name calling and bullying all the time. I was curious and couldn't wait to ask him about Sunday school.

Mum was in the kitchen scowling at us through the window; I think she was angry at Edward for still going out anyway. David turned and looked in her direction, then quickly turned back and said, "Get on with it or she will be out here slapping you."

Dad returned and shouted, "Where is EDWARD?" Mum said, "He's gone to that bloody church thing." "I'll put a stop to that," said Dad. Just a few minutes later Edward returned and the row between them could be heard up the street, but no one dared get involved . Edward was beaten to a pulp and sent to his room. David was shaking with fear and anger, Sarah was crying, and I was shaking. Dad yelled, "Get in here, you three." Very rarely were we called by our names; it was always "you two" or "you three" or "you four," or if on your own, just "you."

Never once did Mum or Dad cuddle or hug us or say "I love you." The distance between us kids and our parents was immense. Two different worlds. We got in the way, a nuisance, children should be seen and not heard, speak only when spoken to. Demands made to witness and do horrible things. They controlled us like robots and contained our rages so we wouldn't tell a soul. They made us ashamed of ourselves and of one another. They isolated us from normality and a childhood. Laughter did not happen in our house. Edward was kept in his room for a few days with just bread and water. His black eyes and bruises subsided and excuses were made for them when he appeared. These excuses were so easily believed by the grownups that we had no hope of telling the truth to anyone.

Dad was still visiting me in the middle of the night. Going to sleep was terrifying, as I knew I would be disturbed by him poking and prodding his bony fingers into me underneath my blanket.

Chanting my times tables and rocking my head on the pillow from side to side, sometimes I would fall asleep, but often

I would just lie there waiting in the dark in absolute fear of what was to come. I would stop breathing just to listen for his footsteps on the stairs or the landing. His stinky breath near my bed. Dad would often scratch me with his nails but I had to pretend to be asleep. His fingers would penetrate and cause me to wince but I dared not move. I faced the wall and his shadow would be on it. The streetlight outside the window gave him such a big shadow. A huge one-eyed monster.

When he had played about enough, he would zip up his trousers and sneak out of the room. I didn't turn in my bed until I was sure he was gone. All the time he was in my room, he rubbed himself with his free hand and made strange breathing noises.

Sleep, please can I sleep now? Scared he might return, I would often wet the bed.

Mum would discover the wet sheets before I woke and rip me straight out of the bed. Dazed, I would hit the floor with a bump and her fist would punch me. Then, not happy with that, she would drag me down the stairs by my hair. At the tender age of nine now, I was a complete wreck.

Most nights after Dad had left the room, I would say a few words to God. At school my teacher told me that God could help you and that he was everywhere. "Please, God," I would whisper. "I want to die, please take me to heaven now. Heaven is for good people, I'm a good girl. Please can I die now? Please make him stop."

CHAPTER 9

# Granny's House

"Mum is not very well and has to go into hospital for a few days, I can't look after you lot, so you boys are going to my brother Steve and you girls are going to Granny." My Granny, I thought. I didn't really know her, as I had only seen her a few times. She was a small lady and my grandad talked funny. Granny smiled as Dad dropped us off. "I will be back to get them on Friday evening," he said. It was a bright but cold Sunday afternoon in December. Granny had decorated a tree and hung paper chains in the living room: it looked amazing. We didn't have anything like this at home. Dad's younger brother was still living with Granny. Uncle Nevil came bursting in and beamed at Sarah and me—I had never seen such a warm smile. Both Granny and Nevil made us both feel so welcome. Granny's homemade lemonade and homemade sandwiches were scrumptious and followed by cake and biscuits. I thought I was in heaven. Beds were arranged in the lounge for us. Nevil came to say good night and turned the lights off; we begged him to leave Granny's lantern lights on as we just couldn't stop staring at the beauty of those Christmas lights. For the first time, I was able to sleep soundly. Granny's house is wonderful, I thought. I don't want to go home, I want to stay here forever. Going to bed with food in my tummy was a new experience for me. I didn't know I could ever feel so good. It was a different world. Granny made sure we were well fed and looked after properly, even sparing time to read to us in the evening. Nevil would appear just before bedtime and stay a while, but I never once felt uncomfortable or scared. He laughed and joked with us and tucked us in. He was a lovely uncle. Sadly he is no longer around; suffering later in life with depression, he took his own life at the age of 28. I have such wonderful memories of him that will always be with me.

After the first night at Granny's, she told us we would be going to school near her house and not our normal school. Granny would walk us to school and Nevil would collect us. Wow, this is too much to expect, maybe I am in heaven, at our other school we all had to walk in all weathers. I remember in the early sixties when I first started school, it was a bitterly cold winter. The snow lasted and lasted but school was not closed. As soon as I started school, Mum insisted I walk. On my feet were jellybean shoes, bright red, and another pair of socks on top to try to keep out the cold. By the time I got to school, my feet would be so painful. The teacher never asked why I was wearing such ridiculous shoes in the snow, snow so deep that it would get my knickers wet. I suffered with severe chilblains as a result. When I got home from school,

### BEHIND BARS

I would rub my feet on the coarse rug by the door until they were so sore I could hardly walk. This school sounded lovely: no school bullies today, no name calling or getting thumped and kicked. "What is the name of this school, granny?" I asked. "Saint Barnaby's in St. Phillips Road," she said. "It's just around the corner and you will be having dinner at school." I love school dinner, we never had food like that at home. Granny gave us such a warm smile as she left us with the head teacher. She was a very tall lady, and as she stooped to talk to both of us she smiled. "Hello," she said, "welcome to St. Barnaby School, I know you will only be here for a short time, but I'm sure you will enjoy it. Class C are making Father Christmas decorations to take home, would you like to join them?" "Yes, please," I said. As we walked through the corridor to Class C I could hear the other children; they seemed to be having lots of fun. As we entered the room, it went completely silent. Everyone stopped and stared at us as if we had two heads each. Both of us stared around the room in shock too, as we were the only white children in the room. At our previous school it was rare to see a Jamaican or Asian child. Looking back now, it was about the time that our government invited many Jamaican families and Asian families to England to fill the shortage of workers; many settled in this country but it did take the British workers by surprise and there was animosity over this. Many workers came out on strike as they believed they would lose jobs to the foreign workers.

## GRANNY'S HOUSE

The look on our faces seemed to alarm the teacher. She came across the room from her desk and spoke to us. "Hello, I'm Miss Brimstone, there is no need for you to be frightened, I'm sure you will both settle in." The head teacher left the room and closed the door. Both of us just could not stop staring at everyone. This upset some of the children and they openly complained to the teacher. "Miss, why is she staring?" After the initial shock had subsided, I was given some green paper, glitter, glue, cotton wool, red crepe paper, and an empty toilet roll. With a bit of guidance I made a Father Christmas and a Christmas tree. I wrote "Uncle Nevil" on the inside of the tree and "Granny" on the Father Christmas.

The bell sounded for playtime. A plump girl grabbed my arm. "I will take you to the playground," she said. I followed her out of the doors into the winter sunshine. The girl let go of my arm and ran off to play with her friends. The playground was small and as I stood there staring at the commotion of the children involved in their different games, I felt a prod in my back. I turned and it was Sarah, still scanning the playground with her eyes. "Are we the only white children in the whole school?" she said. "It looks that way," I replied. Not one other white child did we see in the four days at that school. There also didn't seem to be any bullies. I didn't want to go home; I wanted to stay with my granny and Uncle Nevil. I so looked forward to his smiling face by the school gates at home time.

CHAPTER **10**

# Breaking the Record

Dad came to collect us from Granny's house. I didn't want to go home. Granny's house was so lovely; we even had hot chocolate before going to bed. I prayed the night before by my bed, "Please don't let Dad come and get us, please let us stay here."

Granny opened the door and Dad was waiting—no arms held out to welcome his children, no warm smile, just "get your stuff and get in the car." His harsh look seemed to be a permanent fixture. We did as we were told and said our goodbyes to Granny and Uncle Nevil. As Dad drove off we sat in silence; we both knew we would be home soon, the home I hated so much. I dreamt that night I was still at Granny's with my cup of hot chocolate; wow it was wonderful.

Reality hit me as I hit the floor the following morning. Once again Mum decided to change the sheets and pulled them off the bed with no warning. Sarah also landed with a bump. Dazed and shaken, I picked myself up and gathered up the sheets, then marched off to the bathroom. Mum would fill the bathtub with water and dunk the sheets in a whole box of Omo that was unloaded into the water. The boys had to go through the same twice a week. For most people changing the beds once a week would be enough, but not my mother. I'm sure it was just another way of taking her anger out on us.

When Mum had swished the sheets around a bit in the water, she would let the water out and use the cold tap to rinse the sheets; ringing them out with her hands, she would then put them in a tin bucket and carry them down the stairs to the backyard. The stairs would be slopping wet where she had slopped the water as she walked. Dad had welded the handle back onto the mangle, so in the sheets went through the two rubber rolls; as she turned the handle the water would be squeezed out. Most of the time the laundry would still be full of soap powder. Soon she would be putting it on the washing line.

As the neighbours rose from their beds and carried on doing their bits of washing, she would proudly announce that she had all of her bedding done and pegged out before 6:30 in the morning. I didn't understand why she was so proud of this fact, but it seemed to make her feel good; she would talk over the wire fence to them and brag about her laundry. How nice and white and how she loved to see the sheets blowing in the wind. The neighbours would agree with her. If only they could have been flies on the wall at six in the morning when she was wrenching us from our beds.

## BEHIND BARS

There was no sense to her behavior and no warning of when it would happen again, but happen it did, and it was another reason I was so afraid to go to sleep. Mum didn't have a washing machine—washing machines were rare, and only the rich seemed to have one. Most of my school friends' mums had washing machines. I thought they were all rich; they always dressed in clean fresh clothes and looked happy. Everyone seemed rich apart from us.

Even my cousin May, who lived a few streets away, had a washing machine and a television. Her dad and my dad worked in the same place, there was no difference really, they had four children, so how come they had these things and we didn't? These questions were constantly going round and round in my head. A life of them and us, chalk and cheese. We were different, we had all of our secrets and shame to hide. No one must know, accept it; no one will believe you anyway.

That Sunday, Edward did his usual disappearing act. "Has he gone to Sunday school again?" I asked.

"Yes, I have been talking to Paul," said David, "and Wendy at school, they go to Sunday school. A coach picks them up and they have such a good time. They get big bars of chocolate and bags of sweets. I'm going. I don't care about Dad." "I want to come too!" I piped up. "And me," said Sarah. "When you see the big coach outside, we will go together." We both replied "okay" and put our fingers over our mouths as we whispered, "Just carry on weeding." David whispered, "Don't worry, I will keep a lookout!"

## BREAKING THE RECORD

Time seemed to drag and drag as we pulled the weeds from the garden, the usual Sunday chore. David sneaked around the front of the house at regular intervals until excitedly he came running round the back to say the coach was here. We dropped what we were doing and ran to meet the coach. A friendly face greeted us as we stepped aboard, and off the coach went. Off to Sunday school. I didn't look round at the house, and Mum was asleep in the living room when we left so I didn't think we would be missed.

As the coach stopped at Blackberry Hill, we all piled off and were welcomed into the Church of Pentecostal. Outside pinned to a chalkboard was an LP—or vinyl as they are known nowadays. I wondered why somebody would want to do this to a record; Dad would have a fit if someone did that to one of his.

Inside, lots of people were singing and smiling. The preacher stood and glanced at us. I looked down; I didn't want him to stare at me like that. "We have some new members today," then he smiled. "Welcome, welcome," he said. "This brings our total to two hundred and sixty people." Then he asked us to come forward. We stepped forward and joined him at the front of the church. "You have broken our record," he said as a chalkboard was carried in. "I do hope you enjoy Sunday school, here is a hammer. I would like you to smash the record!" I was very nervous. Holding the hammer I hit the board and the record; it smashed and everyone clapped and broke into song: "Jesus loves the little children, all the children of the world, red and yellow black and white, all are precious in his sight, Jesus loves the little children of the world." A warmth spread over me. This is a nice place, I like it here. Sarah smiled.

The preacher told us to sit down. During that hour at Sunday school we had Bible stories, drawing, painting, and sweets; it was so much fun. Wendy stood up just before it finished and the preacher asked her if she could recite the books of the Bible, the Old Testament.

Wendy chanted them one by one: Genesis, Exodus, Leviticus, Numbers, and so on. I was so impressed. The preacher was also thrilled and gave Wendy a huge bar of chocolate for her efforts and everyone clapped. We all bowed our heads in prayer, and then it was time to go home.

We all had such a wonderful afternoon, I was determined to learn the books of the Bible and see if I could read a bit as well. I was going to get that bar of chocolate next time.

Oh dear, reality check: back on the coach.

We sneaked round the side of the house, hoping that Mother was still asleep and did not yell out for one of us. We did it; she did not know we had even been anywhere. We all planned to do the same the following Sunday; in fact, we managed to do it for four weeks or so. I got my chocolate, and so did David and Sarah.

Then one afternoon as we returned, she was waiting as we stepped off of the coach. God, my heart sank. We all got the hiding of our lives and never dared return to Sunday school again. I still continued to read bits of the Bible that I had borrowed from Wendy. I reluctantly had to return it as it was discovered when the little I had in my room was turfed out and turned upside down. Dad came home that Sunday evening and another hiding was received. He screamed, "I will not have a bunch of Bible bashers telling me how to raise my children." I missed Sunday school so much and begrudged even more those chores of weeding the garden, cleaning, and washing up! Edward continued to go despite Dad's anger. He was so involved and even managed to get a girlfriend whom he later married at the tender age of seventeen. I'm sure now that it was just a way of getting out and maybe trying to forget his traumatic childhood too.

That night Dad came into my room as usual and played around with his fingers under my blanket; once again tears streamed down my face. I had come from heaven to hell in one day.

CHAPTER 11

# The Silver Curlew

"Do you have a black swimming costume and black tights?" asked my teacher one day. "No," I replied. "Oh never mind, I'm sure we could borrow one for you, I want you to be a tree in the school play, *The Silver Curlew*. A letter will go home to your parents asking if you have items such as these and tickets for the play will be on sale at the school." The words "letter to parents" always sent shivers down my spine. Mum could barely read or write; she would just throw it away. If a reply was needed it just wouldn't happen, and the teacher would assume that I had forgotten the letter or didn't give it to my parents. Either way it was always my fault. What was I going to do? "Ping." A lightbulb appeared in my head: ask Pamela! Pamela was a friend at school. She never ridiculed me, called me names, or bullied me. Pamela lived near to our school. Although there was a difference in size between us—Pamela was a lot taller and plumper—this didn't faze me. I was going to ask her if she had a black costume and tights. I could collect it on the way home, no need to take the

## THE SILVER CURLEW

letter home to my parents: a plan was hatched! I knew they would have no interest in buying tickets to see the school play anyway. A few safety pins here and there and I was sure things would be okay with the costume. Sure enough, Pam loaned me black tights and a costume. I told her I would wash it and give it back after the play was finished.

The night of the performance came and the school hall was crowded. I didn't bother looking in the crowd as I knew Mum and Dad had no interest in school plays, or anything I did at school for that matter. All together there were five of us trees, and in practice we had to wave our arms and bend as if it was very windy! This was now the real thing, we had to do this in front of so many people, so I was a bit nervous. We all gathered in one classroom to the right of the stage. A teacher was applying makeup to children who had already changed into their costumes. No one had mentioned that us tree's had to have completely black arms and faces. The makeup teacher approached us with a tray of makeup sponges and water. Panic set in! "Are you going to cover me in black all over?" "No," said the teacher. "First we apply grease to your skin, and then we make you all black!" Still feeling very anxious, the makeup was applied, and quite generously. "Now try not to touch anything," said the teacher. My hands were all black as well as my feet, legs, arms , and face—even inside my ears. My nose started to itch, and as I raised my hand, the teacher shouted not to touch it.

The door opened and the black trees entered the stage. The performance seemed to go on forever, but we trees remained on the stage until the end. All of the parents seemed to enjoy *The Silver Curlew*, so a repeat performance was scheduled a week later.

As everyone left their seats and headed home, the trees moved from the stage back into the classroom. There was no attempt by the staff to help remove the stage makeup. And I was left to walk home from school, totally black.

As I entered the house, Mother took one look at me and grabbed my arm, the black makeup coming off in her hand. "You're going straight in the bath," she said. As she cranked up the old boiler over the tub, she turned to look at me again. "How the hell did you get in this mess?" On the side of the bath were her usual box of Omo washing powder, a bottle of bleach, and a scrubbing brush; these all ended up in the water. The water was piping hot—no cold water was added. Ripping my costume from my back, she picked me up and plunged me straight into the steaming hot mixture. Bleach, washing powder, and the scrubbing started; the bristle brush was pushed hard into my skin. I screamed; the water was turning all of my skin so red. The bleach went into my eyes, and the scrubbing brush was removing the skin from my back. "You dirty little bitch!" she screamed. "How dare you come home like this!" and the scrubbing and screaming continued. My eyes were now bloodshot and sore and my skin red raw! "Oh shut up your screaming or I will give you something to cry about." *Slap Slap Slap!* No one came into the bathroom to see if I was okay or find out what the hell was going on. Mother found it very hard to remove the black paint from my skin and eventually gave up scrubbing. As she dragged me from the bath I banged both knees on the side; grabbing a towel that was like sandpaper, she rubbed me dry. I was in so much pain.

"Now go to bed, there is no food for you!" As I got into bed I couldn't cover up as my skin was so sore, I had to lie there naked to allow my skin to get some air. I had been boiled, scrubbed, bleached, and now totally humiliated. As I lay there with tears streaming down my face, my skin burning with the bleach and the washing powder, I was thinking to myself I want to end all of this, I don't want to live, I want to go to heaven, I want to *die*. Please someone save me from all of this; can anyone hear me? God, can you hear me? God, please save me from all of this. I was only eight years old. I was so depressed and I was so lonely.

That night there was no mercy from my father; he entered my room and fulfilled his sexual pleasure. I was kept off school for a week until my skin had calmed and the redness could be passed off as sunburn. I missed the second performance of *The Silver Curlew*, and for that I was grateful. Mum made some excuse that I wasn't very well and the school accepted that.

CHAPTER **12**

# The Wendy House

Sarah came running to the back garden and taunted me as I'd just got a right smacking from Mum. On this occasion she didn't send me to my room, but ordered me to peg the washing out on the line. My lip was swollen and tears streamed down my face. I let down the homemade clothes prop and could barely reach the line, but I knew if I didn't complete this chore I'd be in serious trouble again.

The sun was beating down and the hot weather made her even more cranky. The slightest thing would set her off.

Down at the end of the garden was a small patch of ground that nothing seemed to grow on. My Mum's voice boomed from the kitchen, "Get that washing out before your father comes home or you will be in for it."

As the words left her lips, he appeared. No smile, no hello—just nothing. He said nothing. After his usual round of sandwiches, he came into the garden and out to his car. He

# THE WENDY HOUSE

returned carrying sheets of hardboard and some long strips of wood. I didn't ask him what they were for or what he was going to make.

He took the wood, nails, and a saw and hammer to the barren patch of earth at the end of the garden.

Sarah piped up, "What are you doing, Dad, what are you making?" "You'll see," he said—again no smile. "Don't get in my way."

A lot of hammering, banging, and sawing went on for a good couple of hours. "It's a small shed," said David. The frame was up and Dad was about to put the sheets of hardboard on for the walls and roof. He left enough room to put windows in. When it was almost finished again Sarah asked, "What is it, Dad?"

"It's a Wendy house," he replied. I'd never heard of such a thing. I remember thinking, is this shed thing for Wendy, or is it someone else called Wendy who we didn't know? I was confused. A house for Wendy? A tiny door and glass windows were put in place the following day. "Here is some old material and curtain wire, I want you to make some curtains," he said.

He measured the wire, cut it to size, and screwed in the hooks to hold them in place, then left the curtain making to me. The material was old and smelled, but I was sure I could do something with it.

## BEHIND BARS

Dad painted the outside walls red and the roof black, a bolt and padlock was fitted to the tiny door, and my newly made curtains hung in position. "Now," said Dad. "I want you to get a ruler and pencil and make the outside look like bricks." The boys had to do one side, me and Sarah the other. It did look like a little brick house by the time we finished. Dad made a small bench to go inside; it did look very good. Sarah was so excited and spent many hours playing inside the Wendy house. When allowed, I would join her; this was after I had done the day's chores first. Mopping the lino, wiping the stairs, mopping the bedrooms, and putting away the laundry.

Like most doors in the house, the heavy-duty padlock was controlled by Dad; the padlock on the living-room door was controlled by him. Padlocks and bolts were part of everyday life. Dad was obsessed with padlocks and bolts.

The little Wendy house had a huge padlock and bolt on the outside. After weeding on Sundays, we would be allowed to play in the Wendy house for one hour. I enjoyed those times very much until things began to change.

Mum had taken a job at our school as a dinner lady. In front of her friends, she would seem a normal caring mum. At lunchtime I would join the dinner line but Mum would not add a bit more food. In fact, the opposite would happen: I would get less on my plate than the other children were given. Some of the children would find this hilarious—that I had less to eat than them—and would make sure I was aware that they were poking fun at me. I knew it would be pointless

## THE WENDY HOUSE

saying anything to Mum about my meager portions of food. As she slapped the mashed potato on the plate, she urged me to move along with a ladle in her hand.

I sat alone to eat my lunch, aware still of other kids taunting and staring in my direction. They sure had plenty to go on. Mum made me wear the knitted jumper that was about three sizes too big, and full of dropped stitches and ladders in the sleeves. Oh yes, they had plenty to pick on me for. I looked untidy and so different from them. Their neatly tied plaits, ribbons, and hair pins—they looked so nice.

Mum would be home before I got home from school, and before I could say a word, she would boom out a list of chores to do. I would always be the last child to leave school at the end of the day, not looking forward to getting home. Other kids would rush past me, so excited to be going home, and sometimes knock me out of the way. Strolling home as slow as I could go. Our neighbours often told Mum that she had the patience of a saint. If only they knew what was going on in our house, I'm sure they wouldn't leave their kids to pop to the shops.

Mum would smile at them and say, "Take all the time you need, they will be fine, leave them here to play." Even on those occasions we would be openly bullied and she did nothing to stop it. With nothing to defend us, she carried on crocheting in the sunshine as though her own kids didn't exist.

When I finally got home from school, Sarah was in the Wendy house playing. We really didn't have any toys to speak of—no dolls or anything like that—so we used our imagination.

### BEHIND BARS

Sometimes we would wash out empty tins and turn them upside down, making holes in the bottom; we'd get some string, then thread it through to make long handles. We made our own stilts and clanged up and down the garden in them. That was until the noise got too much for Mum to bear. She would rush out of the kitchen and snatch them from us, then crush them under her feet. It seemed she couldn't bear to see us laugh or have any fun like normal kids.

She threw the crushed tins into the ash bin and cursed as she returned to the kitchen. That night I was told by Mum that I wouldn't be going to school the following day, as she wanted me to do chores for her, and one day off school wouldn't hurt, would it?

Dad had been working night shifts, and although at home he would be asleep so I had to be especially quiet. My heart sank: home alone with the one-eyed monster. I couldn't think of anything worse; I so wanted to go to school. Suddenly the other kids poking fun at me all day didn't seem quite so bad. Mum would be off to work in the school kitchen at ten and be home by two thirty. I was left at the mercy of the one-eyed monster.

As soon as Mum left the house to go to work, I heard footsteps coming down the stairs. I froze as the footsteps got close: it was him. He looked at me and demanded I make him a cup of tea. He didn't take his eyes off my body, and stared over it for what seemed like ages. I was so afraid, I knew something bad was going to happen. "I want you to bring my tea to

## THE WENDY HOUSE

the Wendy house, and be quick about it," he said. He then disappeared out of the back door and down the garden path. On his trouser belt he had a bunch of keys. He thumbed at the padlock at the tiny door and finally got it undone, then crouched to go inside. As I took the kettle from the stove, my hands were shaking. I had a job to hold it steady as I poured the water into the teapot. I dared not disobey him, as surely I would be beaten black and blue. Walking down the garden path trying to hold his cup of tea steady, the path was uneven but my shaking didn't help. I did spill some of it onto my hand. It burned but I didn't let it show. The tiny curtains were pulled shut; why had he closed the curtains? The panic I felt increased tenfold.

The door to the Wendy house was slightly open. As I pushed it open with my now-scalded hand, Dad was seated on the bench. I handed him his tea and went to walk away back to the kitchen. Before I'd made one step, he grabbed my arm and pulled me through the door, closing it behind me. His hand went above my head and a bolt slid across: I was trapped now and at his mercy.

"I've got something I want to show you," he said. "You mustn't tell anyone about this because no one would believe you anyway, they will call you a liar, and a dirty little liar, you will be put in a home. Come see," he said, his trousers already open and his willy sticking right out of them. He grabbed my hand and held it in place around his willy and rubbed it up and down. "There," he said. "It's not so bad, is it?" His breathing changed. He started to pant a bit. "Kneel down," he said. He pushed my shoulders to the floor and made me kneel still with my hands on his willy. The tears started to flow down my cheeks.

"What are you crying for? It's not as if I have hit you, this won't hurt anyone. No one will know our secret."

I hated him so much for what he was doing to me, but I knew he was right that no one would believe me if I told. They would call me a liar, a dirty little liar.

Dad then grabbed my hair and pushed my head down onto his willy. He put his willy in my mouth and then this salty stuff squirted, hitting the back of my mouth. I gagged and was sick all over him.

This made him angry; he quickly put his willy back in his trousers and ordered me back to the house. By this time my crying was intense. I tried to open the door to escape the Wendy house, but the bolt he'd fixed on was still locked. He slid it open and I ran back to the house, removing most of the sticky liquid from my mouth with cups of water from the kitchen sink whilst still crying.

Dad walked into the kitchen. "Remember, you're a dirty little liar." He then walked through the front room and off upstairs to bed.

I sank to the cold concrete floor sobbing and sobbing. Why did he do this to me? Why? I was so shaken, it took me a while to pick myself up from the floor. Mum would be home and I hadn't done any of the chores. She was going to be angry with me. She probably already thinks I am a dirty little liar. I tried not to cry for the rest of the day, but it was impossible. When Mum did come home, she asked me why I was crying. I made up some excuse that I didn't feel very well. "You better go up to bed then." Without stopping to say any more, I went straight to bed and lay there sobbing.

CHAPTER **13**

# The Move

In a prison, my own prison. I was not disturbed that night, not by Dad or anyone else. Maybe they were told to leave me alone. Dad made up some story about me and they had no choice but to accept it. I was grateful for being left alone, alone in my own confusion and shame. Had Dad decided to visit my room that night, it wouldn't have made a difference anyway, as I was hurt beyond repair. I was a shell going through the motions of living, an empty shell that could cry no more.

My schoolwork suffered greatly as a result of my depression, anger, frustration, guilt, and total shame. Many times at school I looked closely at the other kids. Is the same thing happening to them? I thought. Do they have mums and dads that treat them like Mum and Dad treat me? They all seemed so happy and cheerful, not a care in the world; then I knew I was different from them. A deep feeling of mistrust of all grownups was set like concrete in my head.

## THE MOVE

The term before my eleventh birthday I had to sit an exam at school; the deep feeling I was already a failure made it easy not to worry about doing well and getting a pass. The day had come; the classroom was silent. The exam papers were passed around and a stop clock placed on the teacher's desk. We all sat at our desks and were given instructions, then told to begin. Picking up my stapled pieces of paper and turning them over and over, I looked around the room. Other children were already busy writing. This may as well be a map of Australia—I did not understand a single question. Placing the exam sheet the right way up, I folded my arms. The teacher glanced in my direction but said nothing to me. The time passed quickly and the stop clock buzzed for time up. Not one question did I answer, not a pen mark on the paper. The teacher collected all the papers, then dismissed us all. Everyone seemed to be happy to get out of the room and made up quickly for the time they could not talk. The chatter was loud. "Please leave the room quietly," boomed the teacher. I remained at my desk and was last to leave the room; even the teacher was out the door before me. My blank exam paper, mixed up with all the other papers. I didn't seem to care: I had no spirit left.

Soon it would be time to go home—home to more confusion, shame, and guilt. Was this all my fault? Did I ask for this? My mind was in turmoil.

Soon I would be eleven and going to Penbrook School for Girls. I was a dunce—at least that's what the other kids told me. "You're a dirty dunce," they would say.

## BEHIND BARS

Quite often I would see the girls from Penbrook walking home; they did look very smart with their grey berets and pleated skirts, white blouses with a red and white tie. All looking the same. My current school had no uniform, and I desperately wanted a school uniform to look the same as them.

That summer holiday Mum got some vouchers. She told me they would help with the cost of my school uniform, ready to start school in September. Keith Pople was the school outfitter at the time. I couldn't believe I was going to get some new clothes. Clothes I could wear five days a week. Maybe I would not be treated like dirt or called horrible names when I got to Penbrook School. I will look like them with their new clothes.

On my first day I felt so proud and looked so good. The other kids hated having to wear their grey berets. I loved my beret and wanted to wear it on weekends as well. The other kids would screw them up and stuff them in their bags. I was so proud of my beret and my uniform, one skirt, two pairs of grey socks, the white blouse, a grey cardigan, and my beret. I did feel so good.

There was no name calling or gibes about my scruffy clothes; in fact, the girls who came from my old school could not believe the transformation. P.E. was my favorite time, as I had a new navy P.E. skirt and a white top, as well as new thick navy knickers.

## THE MOVE

The school itself was huge and I often got lost. It would be nice to live here all the time, I thought. How great that would be; no more going home.

The news came out of the blue and hit me like a bolt of lightning. Just as I had begun to make new friends and be treated like a normal kid, the announcement by Dad came out. "We are moving," he said. "We are moving on Saturday, and on Monday you will start a new school."

Once again my heart sank. Dad seemed angry about the move. "We are moving to the other side of town," he said. We kids were not allowed to ask why.

It came to light much later that my dad had lost his job. Sacked from the ironworks; he had been there a long time. My uncle let it slip that he had been fired for fiddling the clock-in machine. I suspect it was probably right.

He was going to start his new job in a bakery. It also came to light much later that as a family we were forced to move because of allegations of sex parties and wife swapping. This was more than likely the reason, so move we did.

Our entire house being so sparse, the contents being fitted into the back of a Bedford van, and off we went to our new home.

I didn't get a chance to say good-bye to my new friends. Our new home was a short walk from the local police station. Halfway down on the right-hand side was an end terrace house. The house had red paint on the bricks around the

## ◄ BEHIND BARS

door and the garden was a mess. The red double gates were broken, but as we stopped in the van Dad jumped out and carefully opened them so that they didn't fall off.

Lots of kids in the street came out and stood staring at us. This made me feel uneasy, the same feeling I thought I had left behind at Longacre School. Dad's friend was driving the van with all of our stuff in it. To unload the van took no longer than 20 minutes as there wasn't very much. Mum had decided to leave the old mangle behind as it was all rusted and the handle had snapped again. The back garden of the house was also a mess. "This house is filthy," Mum announced as she tried the light switches downstairs. She looked at her fingers, and sure enough they were black with dirt and dust. As I walked into the kitchen a mouse ran across the floor; I didn't make a sound as it scurried under the sink cupboard. So used to seeing mice, they really didn't bother me. This house was infested, the same as the one we had just left.

"There is no electric," my mum yelled. Dad was upstairs sorting out the beds. She called again, "The meter is empty." Dad came down the stairs and rummaged in his pockets. "Here," he said, "here put that in." As she took the coin from him she realized she was too short to reach the meter; she looked at him and he tutted. "Give it here," he said. "I hope you don't expect me to keep feeding this thing every five minutes," he ranted. Off he went back upstairs to finish the beds—bunks for us girls and bunks for the boys. Beds passed to us from a member of the family, the mattresses so

## THE MOVE

threadbare that moving in bed would often leave a tear. My bedwetting had worsened, which certainly didn't help their sorry state. Wee-stained stinking mattresses.

In a small bag dumped by the front door were my clothes. I took the bag and rummaged through it, still keeping the contents contained. I couldn't find my beret or my grey skirt, my tie or my gym stuff—where had they gone? My pride and joy. Even though I was no longer at Penbrook School, where was the uniform I was so proud of? Mum seemed to sense what I was thinking as she glared at me from across the empty room. "You won't be needing that where you're going," she said. "I took it back to Pople's and got my money back." A smirk spread across her face; she seemed to enjoy telling me this. "Will I get a different uniform?" "Oh no," she said. "Thank God you don't need one at Conway Road School; they don't have one." Again she smirked. What a strange name for a school, I thought. Then it hit me: I would have to wear my own clothes. None of the children at the school knew me, but I would surely soon become a target once more. My shabby clothes that fit into a shopping bag would surely be plenty to laugh and snigger at.

That night I lay wide awake, thinking how the house so much resembled the house we'd so abruptly just left. I was secretly hoping that maybe, just maybe, some things would be different this time. Hoping that Dad would leave me alone now and that Mum's fits of rage and outbursts of anger and violence had been left behind.

## BEHIND BARS

We had no curtains in our bedroom, only nets up at the window, and outside a lamppost shone brightly. At night I still rocked my head back and forth on my pillow, chanting my times tables on the top bunk and Sarah underneath. The flooring was again lino and very cold; the streetlight made shadows on the wall. I could make a dog with my hands, also a rabbit, butterfly, and a duck. Sarah loved these and we sometimes made up little stories about them. We would have to whisper, though, or we would be dragged from our beds and slapped so hard we wouldn't be able to sit down for a week.

Sarah would often climb the bunk ladder and sit on my bed; together we would play with the shadows on the wall. She sometimes got a bit loud and I was often telling her to be quiet. We would both hold our breaths, so frightened that we would soon hear thumping footsteps on the bare wooden stairs.

My new school was just what I'd expected, only this time, new names I had never heard of came my way. "Look at that, a slut, whore, tramp." I had never heard of these. I was right about my clothes and appearance. They certainly gave them plenty to bully me for. This school was so bad the teachers could not control the unruly kids, and every day some poor kid was beaten up by gangs of other kids. I became the target on more than one occasion. The ring leader, a girl called Sharon, would taunt, steal from anyone, and get her so-called friends to beat them up if they so much as whispered it was her. Her so-called friends were all petrified of her, just her

## THE MOVE

little soldiers who did her dirty work for her and would also take the blame. There were many like her at this school.

The school was split into two schools: girls upstairs and the boys downstairs. Even the entrance to the school was separated by two narrow walkways and a high fence on either side. A big sign stood above the entrance: "Boys" and then "Girls" entrance. To get out of the school we had to walk in single file through the gate; many fights would already be taking place outside.

No one seemed to interfere. The rest of the kids would gather round in a circle as if to shield what was going on from any adults that passed by. They would chant for whoever was winning for fear of being the next one in the circle getting their heads kicked in. Lessons at the school were always disruptive and out of control; fights would break out in the classroom with the teacher in the room. I found school life dismal and pointless at Conway Road.

My wish for things to be different fell on deaf ears, it seems. At home things had not changed either. Mum's temper was even worse than at the old house. Dad, well at night he still woke me. Prodding me and poking his bony fingers under my bedclothes.

One evening as I lay in bed facing the wall, a shadow appeared. It was him; he stood by the middle of my bed. I held my breath, I knew what was going to happen. Pretending to be asleep, I dared not move. The shadows so firmly fixed on my wall, his breathing quite heavy. His bony fingers fondling between my legs and pushing inside me. One hand on his willy rubbing up and down. I could hear every movement. His breathing changed as his excitement grew. Then when he finished, he would rub his sticky hand over my privates and then quickly leave the room. By this time I had learned not to cry. I had accepted this as a part of my life. No one knew about this and I could not tell. No one would believe me; after all, I was nothing but a dirty little liar. I did not trust any grown-ups to be able to tell anyone anyway. Now at the age of eleven, I had a truly dismal existence. Visits from Dad at least three times a week and the routine was always the same.

Life in this house was so dismal. The little visitors got braver and braver, dashing across the room day or night. Sometimes the noise was so loud it was as if there was an army of them. Again mousetraps were laid, and through the night you would hear them snap. It never seemed to make a difference: the more that we killed, the more they seemed to appear.

CHAPTER **14**

# Girl Guides

Mum was obsessed with the cleaning stuff called Jeyes Fluid. This was the answer to all of her cleaning problems. Every room had to be mopped with Jeyes Fluid. The putrid smell of it I hate to this day; the pong makes me physically sick. "Yes," she said, "this will get rid of those unwanted mice, you mark my words." It never worked though, and you couldn't tell her that or she would fly into one of her fits of rage. As she threw a bucket of Jeyes onto the stone kitchen floor and brushed it out with a mop, the neighbours would hold their noses. Kids at school swore I bathed in the stuff; the smell would linger forever on my skin and clothes. By now I was washing my own clothes and ironing them. One thing I never saw Mum do was iron anything; the iron and her had never met. I would wash and dry the same clothes three times a week and try to look after them; it was all I had. They had to be looked after.

Doing the washing from such a young age was easy for me. I wonder how today's eleven-year-olds would handle such a task. Everything done by hand and hard work it was for a seven-year-old; I had already had four years' training. I look back at my sons now and get annoyed at them sometimes because a washing machine is alien to them. This is my fault, I suppose; I went overboard and didn't expect them to do household stuff. I would not forgive myself if one of them felt the way I did when I was growing up.

Although Conway Road was so awful, I still managed to make one or two friends. Sherry was a very tall girl with long blond hair. Sherry treated me differently from other kids; she would always stick up for me when I was taunted and called names. Twice I was invited to her house for tea after school; each time I was so excited. No one had ever asked me for tea at their house, so this was such a treat. Her mum was very kind and welcomed me with a smile. The tea was just lovely: fish fingers and chips followed by jam sponge and custard. Wow, I thought I was in heaven. I didn't want to go home. After tea we went to play in her bedroom. I was amazed how pretty everything was, the beautiful soft carpet under my feet. The plush bedding on her bed and more toys than I had ever seen in my life.

On the back of the bedroom door a very smart uniform hung; it caught my eye. "Yes that's my Guide uniform, do you like it?" said Sherry. The beautiful blue blouse with a yellow neck tie and a shiny shamrock badge. It took my breath away. I touched it and held the fabric with both hands. "I love it," I said to her. I had never heard of Guides and quizzed Sherry about them. "I go to guides on Wednesday," she said. "Would you like to come? It is Wednesday tomorrow, you can come with me if you like, you don't have to join or have a uniform straight away, just come along and see if you like it." "I don't think I will be allowed," I said, remembering all the trouble I was in when I went to Sunday school. I didn't even want to ask whether I could go to guides for fear of a hiding—and rantings about the guide uniform that she had no intention of buying. However I did ask, and to my amazement, Mum said I could go, but still insisted I be back before 8 o'clock even though I explained to her that Guides didn't finish until quarter past. Every time I tried to explain, she would lash out and smack me across the face with such force it would take me off of my feet; I would not get up as I knew a tirade of more attacks would follow. Curling myself into a ball and staying that way until she ran out of steam and left me alone.

The following day at school, Sherry invited me round for tea and said we could go to Guides together; also that she had not one uniform but two, but one was a little small for her now, and if I liked Guides she would be happy for me to have it. I was thrilled. I couldn't wait to go that evening. It was all I expected and more: praise and encouragement to do lovely things and collect badges of achievement. I told Sherry that I loved going to Guides; she smiled, and the following day she came to school with a neatly pressed uniform. I treated it like treasure, my most prized possession. Checking the bag regularly, making sure it didn't get creased up. I couldn't wait to be sworn in as a proper Guide and wear my uniform.

## BEHIND BARS

Mum and Dad seemed to be out a lot more than in lately, and were not aware that I didn't get home until half past eight from Guides. It seemed they had made new friends also. An Asian couple and their family on the next street. Dad would bring home bundles of clothes from this family—these were all new clothes, children's clothes—but we were not allowed to touch them, as Dad intended to sell them. The Asian family ran a wholesale clothing business, and to make extra money Dad intended to sell them. "I want you to try this on," he said one day. He handed me a pink furry jacket. "Put it on," he said. "Do you think you could sell these at school?" he said. "I don't know." The jacket felt so soft. "Well you can borrow this one but don't get it dirty. I want your friends to see it, and maybe they will want one." My school friends already had lovely clothes like this jacket; why would they want this from me?

"On loan"—those words stayed with me. I knew the jacket would never belong to me, or anything nice like this. Kids at school sniggered at me in my pink fluffy jacket. "Where did you get that? Did you steal it or something?" It probably looked that way as the rest of my clothes looked very scruffy. Try as I might, I didn't sell any jackets, and I knew Dad wouldn't be pleased. I was right; he snatched the jacket from me and said I was useless. And that I should go with him to the Asian man's house to find stuff that my school friends would like. I did not want to go with him—being with him was the very last thing I wanted.

70

## GIRL GUIDES

"Go get in the car." I had to obey, there was no getting out of this. My heart sunk to my feet: I didn't want to go anywhere with him. The day before I was given a sponsor form at Guides, and I had left it at home on the kitchen table. The fundraising was to take place at Bath Racecourse; we had to walk round as many times as we could and get friends and family to sponsor us. All of the Guides were looking forward to the event and so was I.

The Asian man's house was just one street away. When we stepped out of the car and entered the house, the Asian family's house did smell funny. The living room was full of boxes, some opened and some sealed. "Have a look at some of this," Dad said, "and see if your friends at school would like to buy any of it." I wasn't interested in any of this stuff and just to keep the peace, I pointed at several items already out of the boxes. "Maybe this, this, and this." The Asian man rubbed his hands together, then reached for his notepad and pen. Dad paid him for several items and then loaded them into the back of the car. "Maybe you can try harder and sell some of these," he said.

As we turned into our street, Dad stopped the car about six houses away from ours. He turned to me and said, "I saw your sponsor form on the table, I will sponsor you and give you lots of money, but I want something in return, I want to have sex with you whenever I want, I don't mean the same as the evenings when I come into your room, I want a lot more." The look in his eyes was so cold; his glass eye was always cold, but his good eye was even colder. I knew exactly what he meant. He continued, "Do you know what I mean?" He went to put his hand between my legs. I opened the car door and ran to the house crying. I went straight up to my room. As I passed Mum, she said, "What the hell is wrong with you?" I said, "Nothing." Dad was going to get his way. It was just a matter of time, and there was nothing I could do about it. I wanted to die.

CHAPTER **15**

# The Bar

The following day as I passed Dad in the kitchen, he whispered, "You tell anyone about what I said I will kill you, do you understand?" I froze in terror; I knew he meant every word. He didn't need to strike the fear of God into me or make threats—I was truly afraid of him anyway.

He did not visit my room for over a week after the incident in the car, but I knew he would be back at some point. The waiting was just as horrendous as the act itself. Not knowing if it was safe to go to sleep. Not knowing when he would suddenly appear at my bed. I learned very quickly not to trust any grown-ups. Grown-ups hurt children: this was so engrained in my head, I didn't know any grown-ups that I could talk to or trust.

Dad had a friend he called Sweeney. Sweeney was a tall man with dark short hair. When Sweeney visited the house we were told to get out of the way. I didn't like Sweeney at all. He had cold dark eyes that seemed to stare at me and made me feel so uneasy. Dad and Sweeney would talk for hours in the front room with a lot of sandwiches and tea on the coffee table. One day I overheard Sweeney telling Dad to hide something. Then Sweeney produced some photographs, which Dad stashed in his shirt. I was peeping through a small gap in the door. Sweeney also gave Dad a piece of paper with a lot of writing on it. "These are the names of addresses of girls who have signed the papers to say I can have sex with them whenever I want. I just give them maybe a couple of pounds for their trouble. Now this list here is from Conway Road School, and, this one is from Merryfield School." I didn't understand for a moment, but then the penny dropped.

I hated Sweeney and Dad so much. They used their power as grown-ups to destroy the minds and souls of children, such as me and my school friends. I listened at the door; it seemed that Sweeney was in trouble with the police. He kept saying things like, "If I get caught with this stuff it will be life for me. *Life*."

Dad hid all of his notes and photos for him and agreed he wouldn't talk to anyone about their meeting. Sweeney never appeared at the house again after that. I was not sorry to see the back of him.

Dad's interest in his photographic hobby increased, and he was developing and printing even more of his own photographs. Some of the material was so disgusting, really not the sort of photos to show friends or relatives unless they were included in his sordid and dirty pictures. Not family album photographs, them.

# THE BAR

In the early '70s it became fashionable to have a bar in your house for drinks and socializing. Dad set about building in the living room a curved bar out of large hollow cardboard tubes and hardboard sheets. It took up one corner of the living room, leaving a small gap at one end so he could get behind it. With some bright yellow flowered paper, he covered the wall and the bar. The flowers on the paper were huge. Not happy that it was finished to his liking, he then decided to stick photographs on the wall in a haphazard fashion, the content of these photos being very explicit. I found them disgusting; so did the boys. We dared not say how we felt about them, though, as we knew it would lead to a massive hiding from him. Was this yet another way of punishing us and driving our shame even deeper within us? Those photographs for all to see. The naked bottom half of my mother with her legs clearly spread wide open, then others of her breasts—close-ups and some taken so both breasts were visible. The pictures didn't vary much; they were all of her and her very naked body. Although one of the pictures went even further: Mother had an object sticking out of her, and her hand was pushing it back between her legs. The ring on her finger gave everything away, as all of the photos had no head. Luckily for me this sort of shame I could keep from my friends, as they never were allowed into the house anyway. I was so ashamed and disgusted at my home and my parents. Dad still visited me in the evenings. His appetite growing ever stronger, his visits seemed to last longer and longer.

This hell continues.

CHAPTER **16**

# Behind Bars

Mum carried on as if the yellow bar in the living room and the photos were all quite normal; even the heavy padlocks on most of the doors she seemed to think was okay. In the opposite corner to the bar, Dad set out building a huge box thing. The box thing had a wide lid that he also fitted with a padlock. "This will stop you lot touching my record player," he said. From the box, he began to thread the wires to the speakers through two small holes he had made, then put the speakers high on the wall; from his bedroom he gathered up his record player and his LPs, locking all of it away in the box. To make it look more attractive as it was just made of hardboard, he wallpapered it with orange flowered paper. It really did look hideous: in one corner a bright yellow bar and in the other, some sort of orange huge lockable box. No one thought it looked okay, only them.

Not happy with these creations he set about changing all sorts of things in the house, making sure everything was under his control with a padlock or two. Sarah and I still had to take our bucket to bed and so did the boys; everything had to be locked down, bolted, and double-checked by him.

The only room without such a lock was the bathroom downstairs. Ironically he took the inside bolt off so that we couldn't lock ourselves in and try to protect ourselves from his sexual advances and his domineering stance. The power he so easily controlled us with.

Having a bath was a frightening experience. Like a predator, he would hover around me until I would take a bath. Many times I tried to barricade the door from the inside so that he couldn't get in. I knew I was really wasting my time. He would hammer on the door with his fists, his voice booming, "Open this door now!" Shaking on the other side, I knew it was a battle I was not going to win; not only the visits at night but going to the toilet or having a bath became a terrifying experience. As he came into the bathroom, the threats would begin first. As if I wasn't already a severe wreck, I was now ordered to get back into what was now a lukewarm bath, and he stood over me with his penis hanging out of his trousers. "There you are," he said, looking down at it. "Someone is pleased to see you." I felt sick; I was cold, shivering, and naked.

He grabbed my hand and made me rub him, then he put his penis to my face but this time I did not open my mouth. He grabbed my cheeks with one hand and squeezed my face, trying to force my mouth open. My teeth remained firmly together. He couldn't control himself, then he covered my face and hair. By this time, another fist was banging on the bathroom door. He dived back against it and zipped up his trousers. The door was opened slightly by Sarah before he had the chance to make sure it was firmly shut with his body. He trapped her fingers in the gap; she screamed and Mother came out of the front room to see what was going on. Looking at Dad and oblivious to her swelling fingers, she just walked back into the front room not saying a word. By this time I had managed to get out of the bath, but no way did I feel clean. I wanted to scrub myself until I bled. I wanted to cut all my hair off as it had some of his stickiness in it. The tears this time did not come; I couldn't cry anymore. The words still echoing in my head: "I will kill you if you tell anyone , you're nothing but a dirty little liar." My body was beginning to change, and he liked this. Sometimes he would say things to me in front of Mum, things like, "I can't get your tits in my hand just yet, but soon they will be big enough." She would make no comment to him about any of the things he said; it was as if all of it was normal. Normal for a father to abuse his daughter. All of their games too, the times stretched out on the sofa on Sundays, her giving him sex and him giving her sex in broad daylight in front of us kids. The shame, the guilt, the depression, the anger, and the sheer feeling of hopelessness. I knew they did not see any of this.

To them it was considered normal, and we had to act as if it was. We had to accept that they could do what they wanted when they wanted; their power and control was instilled in us from a very young age. I was eleven and suicidal; how much more of this could I take before I finally cracked?

When asked if I was okay at school by a teacher, I had no choice but to lie; after all, I'm a dirty little liar. Maybe I should end my life now, he wouldn't be able to hurt me anymore, I wouldn't feel anything if he touched me again.

"What the hell do you want all this iron for?" said Mum. "You'll see," replied Dad. "Mrs. Butcher up the road said she had her house broken into yesterday. I'm going to make sure no one gets into ours," he said. "What are you on about?" she said.

The metal bars looked like they were some sort of iron railings; as he worked with a hacksaw he chopped them into the sizes he wanted. He announced, "I'm going to bolt these to all of the downstairs windows, and then no one can get in." He must have thought it was such a good idea; one by one the windows in the house had metal bars on the inside that he'd fixed in place so that they could not be removed. Even the front door had metal bars running from top to bottom.

Finally all of us were imprisoned not only in our minds but with visible bars to keep us in. I often wonder now what a psychiatrist would make of him. How would they deal with or understand this man's actions? As an adult now I can only think that he was afraid of what the outside world might find out about him, so he barricaded the doors and windows to keep the outside world firmly out.

## BEHIND BARS

It took him two days to cover all the downstairs windows. He seemed proud of his work. "That will keep them out," he said. I could see that Mum was far from happy about this new arrangement. The bars were just wide enough apart so that she could put her hand and wrist in to open the window. None of the neighbours said anything directly to Mum or Dad about the bars on the windows across the street; however, the children found plenty to say about it. It was commonly known by the kids as "the prison." Everywhere I went at school to the local shop, someone would yell out, "Oh there's Lizzy from the prison." Just one more bit of ammunition for a confrontation or a series of name calling. I was now well used to it.

The words engraved on my brain: *prison*, *scruffy bitch*, *dirty slag*, and many more. They just bounce off me and have no effect on my already seriously depressed state of mind. Despite Mum's protests about them, he was adamant about them staying put and getting used to it. Strange how she didn't seem to mind all the photos stuck to the wall in the living room, those very dirty photos. I could tell the bars on the windows made her mood even more difficult to predict.

Mum was drinking a lot more most days; she could down a bottle of gin in an hour or two. Being around her was like waiting for a bomb to go off. I was unaware then that her drinking had always been out of hand. She had always been a drunk. I have been told since that as babies we sometimes were taken from her by a neighbour until she had sobered up.

Dad knew about her drinking and did nothing but encourage her to drink more, bringing home with him a bottle of gin and a bottle of whiskey most nights. The smell of whiskey to this day makes me vomit, as this smell lingered in my room long after he had done his dirty deeds.

CHAPTER **17**

# A Visit to the Doctor

Once again, many of the neighbours' kids had even more to taunt and torment us with. The prison: they joked about it between themselves just loud enough so that I could hear them. We were the source of jokes in the street; it became like a landmark for strangers too. If asked for directions on the estate, "the prison" would sarcastically be mentioned. I did hear this on more than one occasion. A family about to move into the street leading off and close to our house stopped to ask directions. "Oh," said the kids, "you go down the road, past the prison on the left and then turn right." Why did no one from the council question the obvious strange bars on that house? Why didn't the council object to my dad's strange behavior? None of the other neighbours did anything like this.

I began to think we were all abnormal, and I withdrew even more into my shell. The barrier I had built around myself got even thicker. Mum's drinking was now way out of control;

## A VISIT TO THE DOCTOR

constantly in rages of anger she would lash out at the nearest object or person. Being dragged from the sofa by my hair was a regular thing, dragged to the cold kitchen floor with its stench of Jeyes Fluid and kicked and punched until her anger ran out.

One Saturday afternoon I was asked by my dad to fetch something from his bedroom. This was very strange, I thought, as no one was allowed in there. He had a huge padlock on the door at all times. I also can't remember what it was that he wanted me to fetch for him. None of us dared say no to him when asked to do something. We knew it would result in an even more severe beating if we refused. Both of them so clever as not to mark where it could be seen. Oh so trapped in this world behind bars.

My mental prison was also about to get even worse. As he boomed out his instructions, even Sarah and David stopped what they were doing and gazed at me with sad, sad eyes. Am I alone in my total misery? I wondered. Are they going through this hell on earth with Mum and Dad? Just one look at their faces told me that I was not alone, not the only one in this hellhole, going through hell. Neither of them spoke about things that bothered them or upset them; these things they kept to themselves. The pain I knew was just as bad for them. Dad and Mum, however, made sure we didn't talk amongst ourselves about anything. We were isolated from each other, isolated but under the same roof. We grew to mistrust everyone, even each other. Sibling rivalry, I'm sure purposely encouraged by Mum and Dad so that we could not share our thoughts and problems. I'm sure we hated each other; we all had our secrets but could not tell.

"Go to my room now!" Dad demanded. I dared not argue. Opening the door to the living room and out into the hall, I began to nervously climb the stairs. I could feel his breathing on my neck. As I pushed open the door to his bedroom, I couldn't believe my eyes. Mum sat on the bed, and she was wearing the skimpiest baby-doll nightie I had ever seen. Her breasts and lower bits were clearly visible through the garment. Dad was touching my back with his hands and shoving me further into the room. He closed the door behind me. What was going on? My mind was terrified. Bolting the door behind him so that no one could disturb us. I began to cry again; I knew something bad was going to happen. My mother smirked at me. "We are going to teach you about sex, we don't want you to do things wrong when you have a boyfriend." I was eleven years old. I had not the slightest interest in boys.

Still crying, she snapped at me, "It's nothing to cry about, you have to learn." To this day my mother's eyes are cold—the same coldness she showed me in that room. I couldn't speak. I thought I had been hurt more than I could take; I was so wrong.

"Take off your knickers," Dad demanded. Mum looked at me. "You'd better do what he says or it will be worse for you." How much worse could things get? If I had a gun I would shoot myself in the head right in front of them both. It seems

# A VISIT TO THE DOCTOR

I didn't remove my knickers fast enough for his or her liking; both of them leapt at me and more or less ripped them from my skin. "No good crying," Dad said. "You know this is for your own good." I just couldn't believe my ears.

Dad then made me sit on a dressing table, my legs firmly pushed apart. "This is going to happen to you anyway so it may as well be now." Mum made no attempts to stop him as he unzipped his trousers. She started to rub in between her legs and groan a bit. I knew what was going to happen. Mum looked at me and told me to relax. What a sick, sick woman, a very sick mother.

Dad pushed my legs apart and his penis entered me. He pushed it with force. I was in so much pain and the tears were still rolling down my face. He carried on forcing it into me with not a care. The expression on both of their faces was that of sick, sick pleasure.

After what seemed like forever he emptied his stickiness into me. Mum was rubbing herself furiously and making strange noises. Then she said to Dad, "You better not hurt her." Dad had raped me in front of my willing mother. How could he possibly hurt me anymore? His stickiness now running down my legs as I stood up. "No don't wipe it off, you should enjoy it," he said. "This is the stuff that makes babies, but you are not old enough yet to make babies so it is OK." Both of them sick, sick people. Both of them used and raped me. Mentally and physically and emotionally destroyed me.

### BEHIND BARS

Where could I go? As Dad left the room, Mum looked at me and said, "You will not tell anyone or your dad will kill you." "Kill you," she repeated. "Go to your room and stay there."

I had blood on my legs and his stickiness; I was unclean. I wanted so much to scrub myself until I was raw. I knew I would never be able to erase the memory of this. I couldn't wash out my head.

"No you can't go to the toilet," she said; my cries to clean myself fell on deaf ears. "Go to your room," she yelled. Dad disappeared downstairs, but before he left the room he said those same words. "Remember, this did not happen, you're a dirty little liar!" The door slammed behind him.

I thought I couldn't be hurt anymore; I was wrong. Dad had got his way by force; I knew this was what was on his mind when I was in the car with him. What was worse was my mother's face as he carried out his disgusting, dirty, and shameful deed. Only it was me carrying around this burden of guilt—Dad and Mum didn't care about any of it.

In my room I sobbed all night. Not stopping, just reliving the horror of what had happened only hours before. Playing over and over in my head. Seeing Mum's face enjoying the moment. How sick was all of this.

I heard Mum and Dad get up out of their bed and head downstairs. I held my breath listening; I wanted the bathroom so badly. I crept down over the stairs as they talked in the kitchen. Then making a dash for the bathroom and closing

# A VISIT TO THE DOCTOR

the door quietly behind me. As there wasn't any lock, I just prayed I would be alone long enough to have a quick wash—the wash I so desperately needed. The water pouring into the sink was freezing. We were all used to that. Washing in cold water was normal for us. Very rarely did the house have hot water or heating and electricity. Dad was sure as he said he wasn't going to feed the meter every time it ran out of money. So empty it stayed.

Giving myself a very quick wash, I managed to sneak back upstairs without disturbing them. The front door slammed and Dad was off to work. Feeling totally exhausted through lack of sleep and the flashbacks constantly running round my head, I pinched myself hoping that it was just a really bad dream. But no, it was all so very real.

The radio was playing downstairs and *BBC News* came on at 6 am.

Mum's footsteps thundered up the stairs. "Get up," she yelled. "You lot will have me in hospital with bad nerves before long." This was her favourite saying. "I got bad nerves because of you lot," she would continue to rant on and on.

The boys got out of bed first, carrying their buckets downstairs to the bathroom, then we girls followed. "Oh no, not you!" She poked me hard in the shoulder. "Not you, we got to visit the doctor today, you will stay here. You, my girl, are coming with me, no school today." I was horrified. Once more I had no control on what Dad and Mum did with my body; they had already destroyed my mind and soul.

87

Sarah and the boys hurried off to school while I was left with her. "You're going on the pill," she screamed. I found the courage from somewhere to yell back at her, "I WILL NOT!" She slapped my face hard. "YES YOU WILL!" Again I said no, tears streaming down my stinging face. She grabbed my hair. "Oh yes you will, I will beat it into you!" She started *dragging* me down the stairs by my hair as I screamed. The beatings seemed to last forever; I could take no more. Reluctantly I agreed to go to the doctor's with her; I was so destroyed it didn't matter anymore.

It seems Mum had already made the appointment. We sat in the surgery; I couldn't bear to look at her. My name was called and she grabbed my arm. Sitting in the room behind a desk was a middle-aged man. "Take a seat," he said. As he carried on writing something on a piece of paper, he didn't even look up at us. I knew I wasn't to speak. I had already been warned, "You say a word and you will suffer the consequences." I knew only too well what the consequences were. I also knew the reason behind Mum and Dad's demands that I go on the contraceptive pill. I was only eleven years old; was this really allowed?

The doctor finally looked up from his writing. "What seems to be the problem?" he said. He didn't look at me once but focused securely on my mother as if I wasn't in the room. "My daughter needs to go on the pill," she blurted out. "Why?" said the doctor. "Well she had sex with a boy yesterday, and I don't want her getting pregnant." I wanted to hit her, I wanted to hit her so hard until she told the doctor the truth. Still he did not look at me; his gaze was on her, looking as if he believed all that she was saying. I prayed, please look at me, but no.

The chance for me to tell the truth had passed; the doctor asked no more questions and picked up his pen to write out the prescription. "You can collect this at the chemist this afternoon," he said. Before Mum could be asked anything else, she hurriedly left the room, dragging me with her. I wanted to tell him Mum was lying, but those words Dad had imprinted into my head always stopped me: "No one will believe you, you're a dirty little liar."

In the afternoon, Mum picked up the prescription whilst I was made to stay at home. "There," she said, "drink this water and take one of these." She tried to explain that I would have to take a tablet every day. I was having none of it and flung the glass across the room with the raising of my arm. Again the beatings came, dragging me from the sofa onto the floor. "You will take this." She forced a tablet into my mouth and held it shut with both hands. I had to swallow it, I had no choice. "I will do this every day if you struggle, until you get the message."

Mum and Dad's sordid and disgusting games with me would surely carry on if I did what they wanted and took the pill. They would feel quite secure in the fact that I couldn't get pregnant no matter what Dad did to me. This was their plan but it was flawed; the only way I was going to get any peace from the beatings was to agree to take the pill. I was exhausted.

# BEHIND BARS

Mum would bring a small glass of water from the kitchen, hand me the pill, and I would pretend to swallow it; she would make me open my mouth to inspect and make sure. I would hide it at the back of my tongue so she couldn't see. Her eyesight wasn't that good anyway. When she left the room, I would go to the toilet and spit it out. I wanted to tell everyone what both of them were doing to me; I knew I was taking a big, big risk.

On the way to school every morning, I passed the police station. I would stop outside and just stare at the building, trying to imagine the face of the person I would tell one day. Telling all the secrets of our house, just one street away.

The strength to tell, I just didn't have. Where would I go if I told? I had nowhere. Would they send me straight back home? All of these thoughts rushed through my head. Who to trust?

I had learned from a very early age to trust no grown-ups, that grown-ups do horrible things to children. This was like a brass plaque fixed in my brain. Something that will never be erased. Set in concentrate smack in the middle of my head.

Without a clue how to tell anyway and without severe reprisals from my mum and dad.

CHAPTER **18**

# Get a Job

"Lora Phelps has a paper round," said David. "She wants to know if you want a paper round as well. Do you want to come with me and we will see if we can both get one?" "What about my age?" I asked. I was nearly 12 now. David was 13. "I'm sure you and me can get one, we have just got to ask," he said. "You're forgetting I don't have a bike, will I need one?" "I don't know," he said. "Are you coming with me or not?" Mum is out so she won't know. But she won't let me do it, I know she won't. I can't wait until I'm sixteen, then I can leave home. We both left the house and walked to the paper shop, past Melborne Square and up past Broadoake Square. "Where is the shop then, David?" "It's just down there on the right-hand side."

When we entered the shop, a man putting out crisps asked if we had come for the paper round. We both nodded. He smiled and said that the round would be after school for one hour and Saturday and Sunday mornings. For this we

◀ BEHIND BARS

would be paid two pounds ten a week. I was excited at the prospect of earning my own money, and even more excited at spending less time at home. The shop owner stared at me and commented on my very blond hair. At first he seemed a nice man.

"When you are a little older, you can work in the shop," he said. "Someone as pretty as you would be good for my customers." This made me feel uneasy and the barriers around me strengthened. "Oh I'm sorry." He noticed I was feeling uncomfortable about his comments. "How old are you?" I lied about my age and told him I was 13. "Well would you like to start tomorrow? Be here at 6 am prompt and you will be shown the rounds you have to do." Still feeling uneasy in his presence, I couldn't wait to get out of the shop. What was I going to say to Mum? How would she react? I knew I had to tell her about my job.

Whilst she was making the usual round of sandwiches for Dad, I told her about the paper round. To my surprise she said, "Good, you can do that," but then added, "now you can bloody well feed yourself with your own money. When you have given me half of it. You earn money then you pay your way," she snapped. Feed myself, I thought. Well I have been doing that for a long time. Surviving on one meal a day at school for the past eight years. I dared not say this to her or she would have flipped. There is something in it for her; that's the only reason she is saying I could do the paper round.

## GET A JOB

David also had to part with half of his money. She made it very clear that she would collect all the money herself from the shop if we didn't give it to her. She would take it all. We knew we couldn't argue the point.

I enjoyed my paper round and got to know my customers as I delivered the papers. On Sundays the round was very heavy, as all the supplements were added to the already bulky papers. I did my job with a smile. One Sunday, returning with my empty sacks, the shop owner asked if I could babysit for him. "Oh I don't know," I said. I remembered I had lied about my age. "I'm in a bit of a pickle, my wife is in hospital and I have to visit her. Is it possible that you could watch the twins for a couple of hours?" The twin girls were two years old and identical. Sometimes they would run around the shop and giggle at me when I made them jump. I never did tell them apart.

Feeling as though I would be letting my boss down, I agreed to babysit for him that evening, from 7 pm until 10:30 pm. "I will pay you four pounds for your trouble," he said. Wow, four pounds, that's double what I get for a whole week, and I wouldn't be at home; it sounds too good to be true. "Oh," he said, "I will bathe and put the twins to bed, you can sit and watch TV or read a magazine if you want." Even better, I thought.

That evening Mum and Dad were out and wouldn't be back until after midnight. So babysitting for my boss I could sneak out and do.

## ◂ BEHIND BARS

I arrived at 6:45 pm and saw the twins in their jammies. "Say night night," he prompted them, and then he put them to bed. "I will be back about 10:30 pm and I have left your money on the kitchen table." I said "thank you" and off he went, closing the front door behind him. Settling down to watch TV, I turned the volume down so that I could listen out for the twins; amazing, they seemed to be asleep already. Wandering into the kitchen I made a cup of tea, as there didn't seem to be anything worth watching on the TV anyway. Sure enough four one-pound notes lay on the kitchen table. I had never had so much money in one go. Is this really for me? I thought. How could I take this? I haven't earned it, it cannot be mine. Returning to the living room, it was so warm and cosy. I left the money on the table.

The clock on the mantelpiece struck 11:00 pm; no sign of the boss. Where could he be? He said he would be back at 10:30 pm. Just then a key went into the door and he appeared. Looking a bit worse for drink. He struggled to keep his balance and slurred as he spoke. "Everything okay with the girls?" he said. "Yes, everything is fine. Are you okay?" I asked. "Never you mind about that," he said, "you pretty little thing, come here to me." Panic set in, the same panic I had at home. Again I knew something was about to go bad. As he walked towards me he pushed me onto the settee and tried to kiss me; at the same time he had one hand up my skirt, feeling around for my knickers. He was breathing heavily and the stench of booze made me feel sick. I managed to bring my knee up and caught him in the chest; he fell from the sofa onto the floor. I knew I had to get out of there, and quick. Grabbing my small bag on the floor, I fled through the door that he was too drunk to close. I ran all the way home without stopping. My paper round was finished, my job at an end. I could never go back to the shop. How could I face this man again?

The following day David made excuses for me, saying I wasn't feeling well, and by the end of the week he had returned my paper sack.

My mistrust of adults got stronger and stronger. The shop owner had imprinted yet another plaque in my head.

Mum wanted her money at the end of the week, and I had to tell her I had been sacked from my job. I had to lie to try and save my own skin.

"You are not just a dirty little liar, but now you are a lazy dirty little liar as well. You will get another paper round, and you will pay me your dues. Do you understand, my girl?" Although I had lost my paper round, I was determined to get another job. After school I walked into town through the shopping streets and went into every shop asking if they had any jobs going. With no luck, I was just about to give up and go home when a school friend stopped me and said hi. In the gist of a brief conversation, I asked if she knew of any jobs going. To my surprise she said, "Oh yes, try the freezer center in St. Patrick's place. I am doing weekends there." After saying my good-byes I headed in the direction of the freezer shop. Nervous but still determined, I asked for the manager. I knew the first question would be "how old are you?" This was always my downfall as I was very short and people didn't believe my age, thinking I was about 10. Sure enough the manager said exactly that. I could feel my teeth gritting together. But again to my surprise he offered me a job. Packing frozen pies and meat at weekends and after school. The wage would be 15 pence an hour, to rise to 25 pence an hour when I reached 14. Unbelievable. I was so thrilled to get a job that I started the following day. I was now 13; less time at home was what I was after. I would have done the job for nothing, just to stay away as long as possible, so as not to face the dismal life I had there. 15 pence an hour was not a lot, but this was 1972, when the average wage was around £12 a week or so. I didn't care, I had a job—that was all that mattered to me. When I worked, I felt safe from the evil clutches of Mum and Dad.

St. Patrick's Freezer Center only sold frozen products; the work was okay and the staff friendly enough. When I told Mum about my new job, she demanded I give her half of my wages; I had expected as much. "Don't forget," she said, "you will have to keep yourself in food and everything." Once again this was no shock. Mum no longer cleaned or cooked anything, far too busy drinking herself stupid. It was a rarity to see her anything else but drunk.

So excited and longing to work at the end of a school day, I was no longer the last out of school as I had done for many years. During the school holidays I worked all of the days, only having Sundays off. It was great to develop a new bunch

## GET A JOB

of friends—friends that knew nothing about the house that I lived in or my mum and dad. It was great not to be called names like "tramp" or "scruff bag," and being able to buy my own bits of clothes for the first time, and new undies. Wow it did feel good; I treasured each new item like it was gold.

Mum was losing her grip on me and she knew it: I was growing up fast and she couldn't keep up with me. I longed to leave home and have my own space. I remember thinking to myself, when I am 16, I am going to leave home. I mentally ticked off the weeks and months.

As I was spending less time at home, so Dad's attention got less and less. The reason for this, I now know, is that his attention turned to Sarah and David. I was blinkered by my own sense of freedom, and closed my mind to what was going on at home. Sarah began to suffer my mother's drunken rages; she too closed herself into her own shell.

My work at the freezer place carried on for nearly four years. At 15 the news at home came as no surprise to any of us. In fact we were all thrilled, apart from Mum. Dad was leaving; he was having an affair and would be leaving on Friday to live with his new woman. I remember standing in the living room at the point where he was gathering up his things. This was a truly wonderful moment I will never forget. As the front door slammed, I clapped and cried at the same time. My mother was furious at me and raised her hands to slap me. I grabbed both her arms and screamed at her, "You touch me and I will go straight to the police." She backed off. I knew she would

## BEHIND BARS

retreat to her bedroom and drink herself stupid once more. That bastard is gone, there is a God! Thank God for that. No longer would Mum attack me, and no longer would I have that perverted sick bastard touch me. Life was looking up. I had made a stand against Mum as well. I don't know where the strength came from but it worked: she never laid a finger on me after my outburst.

School life was still a struggle and my exams were fast approaching. My boss suggested that maybe I should cut my hours a little to help with the studying. School was not on my mind, though; my newfound freedom filled my heart with hope. My purpose was to leave school and get a job at sixteen, and it couldn't come fast enough. The house without Dad in it was less threatening, and now Mum, permanently drunk, didn't even see half the time who was coming or going. Not able to stand without falling over in her drunken stupor—I found this amusing.

My sixteenth birthday fast approaching now, I began to scan the local papers for places to rent. With some of my wages I started to collect small items for my bottom drawer—flannels, towels, cutlery, tea towels, and little knickknacks to go in my new place. Just before my birthday at school, the careers teacher sat with me, so she said, "What do you want to do when you leave school?" This sort of question wasn't for me. This question was for the brainy kids, the kids that had a life, had a home. Had a mum and dad that encouraged and supported them, listened to them read and helped them with their homework. All of these things and

# GET A JOB

more. I knew I wasn't going to do well in my exams so I expected to leave school with few qualifications and take a low-paying unskilled job. That was me, not what the careers teacher saw in me. My exam results came through and as I'd expected were rubbish. Sitting with the careers teacher once more, she advised I take a job in retail, and that the large department store in town wanted some school leavers. I didn't even have to think about it, I said yes, yes, I would take it. After the interview and tour of the store, I was due to start work on the Monday after leaving school. Great, this is what I wanted, now to get cracking and scan the papers properly. Find myself a home—nothing else was more important.

Bedsits were all the rage then. *Bedsits available for rent, local area, viewing to take place on Sunday at 3 pm and number 55 Station Road.* I was definitely going to be there, no matter what. The rent was £4 per week. My wages at the superstore were £7. I could afford the rent, not having to share my wages with Mum. Yes, this was for me! Turning the corner of Station Road, I couldn't believe my eyes: there was a queue of people waiting for the landlord to arrive. I thought I was early, and naively had expected to be the only one viewing the bedsit. I joined the queue, feeling slightly hopeless. All of these people, couples and couples with babies. My heart sank. Did I stand a chance?

As the queue started to move, I listened to some of the conversations: the top floor is empty and the ground floor, the basement flat is empty. Realising then that maybe I was in with a chance, the queue slowly began to disappear. There was no one behind me; I was the last. Mr. Milson, the landlord, held out his hand to shake my hand as I entered the house; taken aback by this and feeling very nervous, I stretched out my hand to shake his. "All of the other rooms are taken, I have this one left." His hand turned the brass knob on the door. The room was very strange but spacious with large bay-type windows and old sash cords. The ceiling was painted in bright yellow, the walls blue, and the door orange. Not a bit bothered by the décor, I knew I could change all of this anyway. "The electric meter," he said, "is there on the wall. It takes 10 p coins so you must make sure you don't damage the meter."

What he meant by this I had no idea. In the corner left of the window was a sink; it looked like it needed a good clean. "I expect a deposit of £4 and £4 rent in advance." This was not a problem, as I had saved every penny for this moment. This little room that I would make my palace, my safe place, my safe retreat. Mr. Milson wanted an answer there and then. He asked if I was working, as he didn't accept anyone into his bedsits who was unemployed. "Yes," I said, "I work in the centre of town at the superstore." "Well then, do you want this room or not?" "Oh yes," I said, and handed him the rent and deposit.

To my surprise he produced a written receipt. "I will see you in one month for the rent, here is your rent book, if you are not here I have a key, leave it for me."

We shook hands once again, and he handed me the keys to the main door and the room. I couldn't believe that I was last

# GET A JOB

in, but had the keys to my very own place. I left with the keys in my hand. *Thrilled* is not a big enough word to describe how I felt that day. Absolutely ecstatic and overjoyed. The start of my new life—a set of keys away.

I couldn't wait to tell Mum I was leaving. I went over and over in my head things I would say, trying to put the words together, all the years of hurt, and now they would come to an end. I would wave the keys at her and not even say good-bye. I held the keys very tightly in my pocket, I was afraid to let them out of my fingers. This is my future now, this is me, I can live my life.

Mum was in the living room when I arrived home. She looked at me and said, "What are you smirking about, I will wipe that smirk off your face now if you like!" "I have got something to tell you, Mum, and you're not going to like it, but you know what, I really don't care." I could tell once again she was so drunk on the gin. "But before I tell you there are a few things I am going to get off my chest." I took a deep breath, and out it came. "I never liked you as a person and as a mother, you don't deserve the title, you shouldn't have had any children, you never loved or cared for any of us, the day Dad left was a brilliant day for all of us, he used, physically, sexually, and emotionally abused, all of us. With your encouragement. Both of you are sick people, you didn't care that what you both did was so wrong, you at any time could have stopped it but you did nothing, you are both evil people." She ran at me with both fists aiming at my face. "I am leaving today, I no longer want anything to do with you or this house." Her fists dropped before she got to my face. "Yes I am leaving today, you will have no more of my time or money, Mother." I waved the keys in front of her face, and she stepped backwards, not speaking.

As I left the room, she remained silent. I made my way upstairs to my bedroom and collected my items from the bottom drawer. My contents just filled three carrier bags, including my clothes, at the bottom of the stairs. Mum stood waiting for me, slurring as she spoke. "You don't know what I had to go through," she yelled. Yelling back as I left the house, "You had a choice, Mother, we were children." I jumped on the bus after leaving the house, still filled with anger, and made my way to my new home in Station Road.

I jumped off the bus just a few hundred yards from the house. I put the keys in the door, five coins into the meter, and sat on an upturned crate that was in the middle of the floor.

This was my own heaven. The years spent here turned out to be some of the best years of my life.

CHAPTER **19**

# A Knock at the Door

Suddenly jolted back from my memories by a knock at the door: *tap tap*. "Hello," a high-pitched little voice spoke; realization set in quickly that on the other side was a policewoman. As I opened the door, my hand was shaking and my heart was pounding. "Elizabeth," she said, slightly stooping forward as I answered with a stutter, "Yes, that's that's me." "I didn't know what door to knock on as there are a few. Trying to raise a smile and to hide my nerves, I agreed. "Glad you chose this one, I can't hear a thing if someone knocks at the front." The woman held out her hand. "I am PC Miles from Avon and Somerset Police, may I come in? I have never been to your town, what a strange road layout." After shaking her hand, I invited her in and asked her if she would like tea or coffee. "That would be very nice, yes, tea with milk and no sugar, thanks." "If you would prefer, you can call me Linda." "I can see you are a bit uneasy, but please try not to worry." I asked her what this was about, knowing full well and dreading her answer. Placing the tea on the table, I sat quite awkwardly on a chair opposite her. "I am here because your brother David has made very serious allegations about your mother and your father. I have come to see you to ask if you know these to be true?" There was a long pause... "Are you okay?" Without any warning I just burst into tears. Again she asked whether I thought there was any truth in these allegations. "Okay we will take a minute, I can see something I have said has upset you." I tried so hard to stop the tears but still they kept coming; this poor policewoman I'm sure was not expecting such raw emotion. Finally managing to control myself, she asked again. "Your father has been arrested." I wanted to scream at the top of my voice, "YES!" I know that David and Sarah had also suffered at the hands of both Mum and Dad. Out of my mouth poured years and years of hurt and anger. The woman did not know what had hit her and wasn't sure how to react. Now to a total stranger, I was releasing all of my disturbing childhood, and that of my brothers and sister. She was a bit overwhelmed with all of the information and suggested we take a break from this informal interview. She talked about her job and how David made the call to the police, still very anxious and distressed and knowing full well what was going to happen and the course of events that would unfold. I had been waiting my whole life to unburden myself from my past, and the opportunity was sitting at my dining table. Don't let this slip by, I thought; my heart was telling me to do the right thing. The woman asked when was the last time I had seen David or even spoken to him. "It has been at least 22 years," I replied. "Your father is saying that *he* is making all of this up to ruin his reputation." I knew

# A KNOCK AT THE DOOR

this wasn't true. "This is going to be very difficult to prove otherwise unless you are prepared to make a statement." I was terrified about all of this.

Leaning towards my sideboard, I opened a small drawer and pulled out the notepad I had been reading through before she arrived. The A4-size notepad was full of my handwritten notes. I handed it to her. "What is this?" she asked. "Two years ago, I started to write about my childhood, I had read in self-help books that it would help me to overcome the pain of my past." She was not expecting this and was amazed at the detail; within its pages, there was everything she could possibly want to prove my father's guilt. "Can I take this?" she asked. "Yes, but I would like this back when you are finished with it." "That may be quite some time," she said. I asked about my sister. "Have you seen her or spoken to her?" I already knew the answer would be yes. I asked what Sarah had said. "She also said that things were not right when you were children; we have also spoken to your older brother, who said none of this ever happened." This made me very angry, as I knew he was lying. He didn't want to tell the truth; maybe it was just too painful for him to drag up. After all it was forty years ago. We had all tried to move on with our lives; this was very painful for me having to relive every bit of it. The pictures still vivid in my head. The policewoman left her card and said she would be in touch soon. My eyes were still full of tears. My youngest would be home from school soon—better pull myself together, and fast. I don't want him to see me like this; also back to work tomorrow where I have to try and act normal and smile. So much was running through my head.

Sleep didn't come that night, the nightmares of the past resurfacing. Just before work the phone rang. "Liz, it's me," a voice at the other end announced. "Sarah." "Yes it's me, the police have just left." She was crying. "What did you tell them?" I asked. "It's all true, it's all true," she blurted, still sobbing. "It's all out now." "I know," I said. "Will you make a statement?" Both of us were unsure. I replied, "I have done nothing but think about it, I cannot sleep, I have to go to work now and pretend everything is okay. I don't know if I can do it but I will be home at 10 pm, will you call me back then?"

My shift started at 1 pm. I tried so hard to shut out what had happened in the last 24 hours and be cheerful, but it didn't work.

The hot deli counter at work was busy as usual, and my workmate Sheila noticed I wasn't my normal self. I couldn't tell her anything, she wouldn't even begin to understand. The day was a huge struggle; I spent most of the day avoiding customers and staff by washing pots at the back of the deli out of view from everyone. As soon as I got in the door at home, the phone rang. "Liz, it's me, the police know everything, I told them, and I'm scared," she said. "I'm scared too," I replied. "I struggled at work today and Sheila kept asking if I was okay but the words just wouldn't come out. I don't know what to do, my mind is saying forget the past but my heart is saying to do the right thing. I think I'm going to do the right thing. I know I haven't spoken to David for many years, but I will make a statement, for all of us—this is for all of us. To be able to get the truth and to have closure on the whole thing is the right thing to do." She paused for a moment. "Are you at home on Tuesday, it's your day off, isn't it?" I replied simply, "Oh yes." "I will come and see you, we really can't talk about this over the phone." "Okay, I will see you then," and then we both hung up.

Tom was staring at me in the kitchen like I had two heads or something; he guessed that something was not right. My husband and father of my five sons—where do I begin? Years ago I did say to him that I was abused, but he didn't really listen. I didn't go into any detail. Our marriage had been extremely rocky, and his drinking was, at times, unbearable. The physical abuse towards me made me dislike him even more, and his general attitude towards me was cold. I didn't want to tell him anything, I didn't trust him at all; he had already given me plenty of reasons not to trust him. I don't even know why we were still together. It's like we were two strangers living in the same house. I cooked, cleaned, and took care of the kids, worked to provide and pay the bills. He had his own life, this was obvious—his own agenda. He didn't support us, all of this I had to do. I was totally fed up with our marriage and told him it was a sham and a lie. Many times I would tell him all you want to do is drink, and we won't go into the adultery side; for the sake of the children we stayed together, although I'm not sure this was a good idea. The boys had seen firsthand his drinking and his violence. I suppose I thought I could change him. Someone should have shaken me 20 years ago and said now is the time to quit. His life and mine couldn't be more different: abuse to him was a pinch on the backside, and he was not ready to listen. Even though we had stayed together for 30 years, he always avoided anything that was uncomfortable and difficult to talk about. He would be eager to give advice in his military manner, but he was never really listening. Why we were still under the same roof was a mystery. Even that mystery would be solved.

He did the honorable thing of giving me babies, but I had to raise them as Mum and Dad; he had very little time for us all. Some men get jealous when babies come along—they take a lot of looking after—and I think he was one of these men. If I sound bitter about him, it is because at this time, I was both angry and bitter. He would preach family values but never practice what he preached. Many times, being drunk, he would accuse me of having an affair. Nothing could be further from the truth, the truth being I would cringe when he touched me; I would feel vulnerable and scared. He didn't want to understand, and the more abusive and drunk he would get the more I hated him. I yelled at him one evening, "I wouldn't have another bloke if every hair on his head was a diamond." He would never understand my fear of men. I can now admit that I was scared of men.

He was watching me as I put down the phone. "What is going on?" he snapped. I replied, "It's nothing to do with you." The phone rang again; he was quick to pick it up when it rang the second time. "This is PC Miles, may I speak to Elizabeth, please?" I could hear her voice on the phone. "Why do you want to speak to my wife?" he snapped. "It is personal, please may I speak to Elizabeth?" she continued. By the look on his face he wasn't too happy about this call but handed me the phone anyway. "Hi this is PC Miles, can I come and see you on Wednesday next, I believe you told me it's your day off?" I said yes it would be fine. "Have you made up your mind as to giving a statement? All of your notes are extremely helpful and will be used as evidence against your dad should you want to proceed. I will be keeping them for a bit longer." "Okay," I replied, being careful not to say too much on the phone or give anything away to Tom at this time. "I said yes to your previous question and I will see you on Wednesday." As I put down the phone, I could see he was very irritated. "What's going on?" he said again. "I don't want to talk about it right now." He seemed to accept this but I knew it wouldn't last and later he would want to know the truth. Where the hell do I begin? I thought. He didn't want to know when I tried to tell him before; was there any point in talking to him now? Things kept popping into my head. My notes: he knew nothing about them, and I knew I wouldn't be able to keep them from him.

Another restless night in store. I wanted to be left alone, I did not want to talk, but he has his way about him, he seems to force words out of me. I answered his questions in one-word answers. "Please, I want to sleep," I begged him. "Let me try to get some sleep, I have got a lot on my mind and you're not helping." But he would not take no for an answer.

"Okay, okay, I will tell you, David has gone to the police about abuse... Yes," I said. "You heard me, and he has made a statement, Dad has been arrested, Sarah and Edward have had visits from the police too, I will be seeing PC Miles on Wednesday to make a full statement and I have said I will go to court. Please now can I get some sleep, or try to?"

He was horrified. "Why didn't you tell me all of this before!" "I tried to tell you about the abuse years ago but you didn't want to know, you were drunk as usual. You even said I must have asked for it." "No, I wouldn't have said that!" "Oh yes you did, I remember how hurt I was. That I couldn't even tell you without ridicule and nastiness, you didn't want to know, and I vowed I would never say anything about it again." He was upset by these words.

"I have been a right bastard to you, I know I have, I will leave if you want me to... I will leave tomorrow." For the first time in our marriage, the truth was finally coming out. "I don't deserve you I know and if you say it's over, I won't like it but I will accept it." At that moment I was ready to throw in the towel, to give up.

The morning came; no sleep again. He left the house none the wiser as to what I had to go through, and again in his blasé manner brushed it off. At work again I struggled with the most menial of tasks. Sheila became even more concerned. "Look," she said, "I know there is something wrong, you can tell me. Come out the back and tell me, I won't say a word." "Sheila, it's very complicated," I said, "but I think me and

## A KNOCK AT THE DOOR

Tom are finally over, he will be moving out. Things are not what they seem and it's best for both of us. I need some space to deal with something and I can't deal with him as well. I asked him to go, he is moving out on Saturday." Sheila was shocked. I did not say anything about the case, the police, and the allegations; that would have been too much to handle in one day. Whilst trying to wash up the silver trays, I burst into tears. She didn't know what to do; she left me at the sink and carried on with her work. The burden I was carrying was immense, and took over every minute of my time. I tried to keep busy and block it out, but the minute I stopped the memories chased me like a big black cloud in a strong wind, moving so fast. Wednesday came so quick and a knock at the door. PC Miles put her face round it as it was slightly open. "Hello," she said, "is it okay to come in? Is there anyone else in the house? We can go somewhere else to do the statement if you wish so we are not disturbed by anyone?" The last thing I wanted was for any of my children to hear what I had to say, but knowing the house would be empty for at least three hours I assured her we would be okay. She filled me in with a statement layout, and how the questions would go. She assured me that it shouldn't take longer than an hour; I don't think she was expecting quite a detailed statement. These sharp images still in my head after all these years. The effects on me, the depression, the guilt, the anger, the shame, all came spilling out. Spewing like a poison from within me. When she left after two hours I was so exhausted but somehow felt different, as if a new spark of life had been lit deep within. The spewing of all this poison that had been kept hidden within me for all of my life—maybe I would finally begin to heal now.

Tom rang me that evening and asked me how it went; I was surprised he was even interested. Sarah rang shortly after and said she too had made her statement. Our evidence would be enough to charge Dad with serious sexual offenses. I prayed it would be enough; if he had walked free after giving my evidence, I was scared he might come after me. The threats he had implanted in my head flashed right to the front like a beacon.

Dad was charged on that Friday afternoon and released on bail.

Tom was here when the phone rang; he'd popped in to collect more of his clothes. My shift at work had ended at 4:30 that day. I had just got out of the bath at 8:00 when downstairs I could hear the phone ringing. He picked up the phone. "It's for you," he yelled up the stairs, "it's that PC Miles again." Quickly putting on my wrap, I came down the stairs and taking the phone from his hand I said, "Hi, can you give me a minute?" I grabbed a piece of paper and a pen and walked into the conservatory. "Are you okay?" she asked. "Under the circumstances, no," I replied, "but hey you still have to go on, don't you!" She continued, "We have charged your father today with 72 offenses and feel sure that the Crown Prosecution Service will take the case to court. Will you testify?" There was a pause. I replied, "I have made a statement so I will testify." "Your sister will also testify if you do. Your father is being charged with…you might want to write this down.

"20 counts of indecency with a child,

A further 20 counts of indecency with a child,

One of rape of a child under 12,

A further 20 counts of gross indecency with a child,

A further 11 charges of gross indecency with a child."

"Please can you slow down, I'm trying to note this all." I was in shock, I never thought this would be so big. I didn't really know the whole truth about my brothers and sister, but obviously there was a lot more than just me. She then added, "He still denies that anything ever happened and that all three of you have concocted this story to ruin him. He says he has had a good life and you just want to spoil it and you're after his money.

"I know you made a statement, but would you be prepared to make a video statement as well? This would be shown in court and you may not have to appear." Still trying to get my head around all of this, I agreed. Oh my God, this is huge. All sorts of things now flashing through my head: the papers, it's all going to be in the papers, everyone will know, the TV, the local news, this is a small town, the *Weekly Times*—my brain was doing overtime. The boys will be affected by all of this. I need to get them together and tell them the truth before some of their friends spread the gossip. Tom was looking at the piece of paper on the table; he picked it up and read what I had written. Pulling out a chair with the paper in his hand he sat; putting the paper down, he placed his head in his hands and cried. I had never seen him cry before. As he sobbed he said, "I didn't understand, I didn't know, I love you and I'm sorry, I am so sorry for everything, had I known I would never have raised my voice at you, I love you so much can you find it in your heart to ever forgive me? I hope so. I hope we can still be friends if nothing else, I am sorry I didn't know how bad things were and how stupid I have been, everything is now clear to me I understand now, I have been such a bastard. How the hell have you managed to cope hiding all of this for forty years? How did you survive from day to day, how did you cope with me as well? If I could take back the time and give it to you again, things would have been so different for you. I know now that you are my life, without you I have nothing, I am no one, you have been so strong for everyone, I am so, so sorry." Trying to still focus on the piece of paper blurry eyed, he said, "This piece of paper has changed my life, this is like a gift from heaven, the biggest wakeup call I will ever get. I will still stay away, and I now understand why you need the space, I really do. This is huge; you are so strong to be dealing with it and try to carry on as normal, I still would like to support you through this, and if you want me to come to court with you I will, and if you want me to stay away I will."

This person talking to me now is not someone I know. This is the man I wanted for thirty years. This man is pouring out the truth to me; he was in a deep state of shock at the severity of all the charges. "You can help," I said. "In what way?" he replied. "I'm going to be in working away , how can I help?" "The police want you to make a statement, she wants to know if I told you I was abused as a child, here is her number; you can give her a call." "I will do it, I will do whatever it takes. I will make a statement. I will try," he muttered.

Tom came to the house to make his statement. PC Miles said she would be in touch with me soon to make the video statement she had previously mentioned. Every time he came to see me, he would burst into tears and so would I.

"I thought you were having an affair, you wouldn't let me close to you so I drank, I was very frustrated, I now know why you were this way, I didn't understand, I'm not trying to make excuses for myself, I don't have any, I love you and always have, you are that little blonde who I fell in love with and I know I didn't treat you right. Give me the chance to change that now. I'm begging you please, please give me a chance." Tom had never spoken to me like this before and I was lost for words. I had a lot of thinking to do. Not only dealing with all of this but our relationship too; it was all too much.

The following Wednesday PC Miles collected me from home. As we drove away from the house she turned to me and said, "Would you be more comfortable calling me Lin?" "I think that would be much better," I said as we continued our way to the safe house. On the way she explained, "We use this house for our video evidence." As we entered the house it looked like any normal home. I sat in the lounge. Lin, for once, made me a cup of tea. It was very hard to talk about my abuse and having to go into such detail using words I am very uncomfortable with, to say the least. I was glad when the whole experience was over. Lin drove me home. My house was buzzing with the boys and Tom. He stopped talking to the boys and asked me how it went. I said okay; I lied. I made a tea and went upstairs, placing my tea on the dresser. As I lay on the bed the tears came uncontrollably. I didn't want anyone to see me like this. I stayed in my room for the rest of the evening, just as I had done so as a child. In fact during all of this, I found myself doing things I did when I was eight years old to protect myself from the hurt, rocking my head from side to side on the pillow. I really thought I was beginning to go mad.

CHAPTER **20**

# The Case and the Trial

The police had arranged for me and Sarah to see a counsellor. We would be assigned a counsellor from Next Link. Next Link's funding came straight from the police. Dee introduced herself when she came to see me at home. All through the trial she was amazing; I could tell her anything and she wasn't going to judge me or think I was some crazy woman. The first time I met Dee I broke down in tears; everything poured out the way I was feeling about my marriage also. She just listened; she did not judge or tell me what I should do— finally someone I could trust with my thoughts and feelings. "I will be there every step of the way," she said. I found this very comforting, as I'd never had anyone I could rely on before and truly trust. Through Dee I was told that David had been offered counseling, but he had refused. I still had no contact from him, no address or phone number. I so wanted to let him know that we were behind him and were going to testify. I hoped that Dee could pass on a message through the police; I wanted him to know he was not alone in his turmoil and stress. We would be there for him, and I know and felt everything he was going through.

Work was becoming harder to cope with, the stress so obvious on my face that again Sheila persisted. "I know you have got something on your mind, tell me, talking might help." "I don't want this going further, okay! My brother went to the police about things that happened to him, well all of us kids. Dad was arrested and we have to go to Crown Court. "Oh my God," she said. "What are you doing at work, how are you coping with all of this?" "I'm not coping very well, Sheila, I am waiting for a date for the trial to start so I can arrange time off to attend, I have said I will give evidence so I have to go."

"First Tom and now this! Oh my God, can't you take some time off, how can you work with all this on your mind?" "It's work keeping me going at the moment, without it I would crack and fall to pieces." Sarah suggested staying at her house during the week of the trial, so I wouldn't have to travel for two hours every day to the court. The trial date was set for the eleventh of November: official notice came through the post. Tom had also received a letter to appear as a witness. I wasn't sure how he would take it and whether he would go or not; it had to be his choice and for the right reasons.

Luckily it was half term the week of the trial so my youngest could come and stay as well, keeping Sarah's two boys company. I arrived at work holding the letter from the court in one hand. "Hi Sheila, have you seen the duty manager?"

## THE CASE AND THE TRIAL

"Yes, she is on the counter." I wandered over. "Can I have a word, please?" "Go ahead, I'm all ears," she joked.

I felt very uncomfortable. I didn't want to discuss the details of my letter on the shop floor. "Can we talk somewhere else, please?" "Oh, okay," then I followed her into the security office and she said, "Sit down, what is this about?" "I have a letter from the Crown Court and I need some time off from the 11th of November." "Have you been a naughty girl?" she joked again. "No, I am a witness in a very serious case." "Well," she said, "I don't know if I can give you the time off." This time I knew she wasn't joking. "I have been told by the police that if I do not attend I will be arrested at work and taken to the court, you have no choice but to give me the time off." She replied, "If as you say they come and arrest you, I won't let them until you have finished your shift." I couldn't believe my ears and she was deadly serious. Reluctantly, she decided it would be better if she just gave me the time off without pay. I had to settle for that.

That afternoon Sheila asked if I had a date for the trial. I said, "Yes, the 11th of November. "Oh, so close," she said. "How are you feeling?" she asked. "I'm petrified." All of the girls on the counters looked at me a bit odd. I knew then that she had told them everything. I was a bit hurt by this but then realized, well everyone will know soon anyway so what the hell.

The next few days I didn't stop crying at work. I decided it would be best if I stayed out of sight at the back of the hot deli where I couldn't be seen by the customers. The days seemed to go very quickly getting closer and closer to the trial.

On Sundays I work from 8 am until 4 pm. The Sunday before the case was a huge struggle for me; I was finding it so hard to raise a smile at work, didn't sleep at all again the night before. The girls tried to cheer me up, but I really wasn't in the mood; the pressure I felt was enormous. My shift ended and I said good-bye to the girls. As I was leaving the counters one of the girls raised her head and said, "Good luck for next week, I hope it goes well for you." She put her arms around my neck. I just burst into tears and tried to thank her through my blubbering.

When I got home, my youngest had already packed a small travel bag with his clothes and electrical extras (phone, iPod, etc.). I didn't have time to be fussy so I threw some clothes in a holdall and left for Sarah's house. As I was about to close the back door, the phone rang. I dumped my bags onto the kitchen floor and grabbed the phone. A little voice said, "Hi, this is Lin, can I speak to Elizabeth?" "Hi, it's me," I said. "I didn't really want to bother you on a Sunday but something has come up. I have been instructed by your barrister that it would be beneficial to view your video evidence before you take your stand in court. Is it possible for you to do that today?" "No," I replied, "I am on my way to stay with my sister until the trial is over." "Oh that's okay; I can pop it round to her house first thing tomorrow morning. There will be no need for you to attend court on Monday, I agreed to do just that, and then I will see you at the court on Tuesday morning."

## THE CASE AND THE TRIAL

Forty-five minutes later I arrived at Sarah's. The phone was ringing as I tapped on the door. Her boys greeted my youngest as if they hadn't seen him for years; Sarah appeared with the phone still at her ear. "Just a minute," she said on the phone, "she has just arrived." I placed my holdall down in the hall and took hold of the phone; it was Tom. "I will be with you every step of the way, I will pick you up at eight in the morning so you don't have to take the bus. Lin rang me before I left and told me we don't need to be at the court on Monday, so Tuesday would be better, I want to be there I need to know the truth, I love you so much you are so brave." He then hung up. Sarah then appeared with a cup of tea. I still had my work uniform on—in the rush I had forgotten to change. I could tell she had been crying. I took her hand. "I know you are really scared and so am I, but together we can do this." She nodded and wiped her eyes with the back of her hand. That night she told me what Dad had done to her; I knew he was up to something with her but we never talked to each other as children. For the first time in our lives we really talked. Everything seemed different; sharing our past was a release. The boys disappeared to their rooms to play games, and we didn't see them for the rest of the evening. "Why didn't you tell me when you came to my bed-sit?" I knew the answer to this of course: the threats. The threats he'd made to her were probably the same as those he'd made to me. "We had better try to sleep, it's going to be a long day tomorrow."

The doorbell rang dead on 8 o'clock. I was expecting Lin to bring my video evidence, but this was a different policewoman.

"I am from the local police station, are you Elizabeth?" "Yes," I replied. "I believe you're going to court tomorrow and you have to view your video evidence before you go; can I pop it in here?" As she reached for the DVD player under the TV the boys were upstairs, so Sarah told them to stay there until the viewing was over. "I will stop this at any time if you wish and take a short break," she said. Sarah disappeared into the kitchen and closed the door. The content of the video and my evidence made me cry; Sarah had already placed tissues on the sofa. I didn't realize it was nearly an hour long. It really did upset me, the things that came out; had it been a stranger telling of these horrible things, I still would have been upset. I found some of the things I was saying hard to believe, but they were all true. Then it dawned on me even more how serious all of this was: this was not a stranger, this was me telling it how it happened and using words I wouldn't normally use to describe what that bastard made me do. My mother's part in all of this I mentioned too; who would believe that both a mother and a father could do such things to their children, but it was all true. I cried and cried. I knew my mother would not be called to court as a few months earlier she was diagnosed with dementia. Her short-term memory loss would act as her saviour, as she couldn't be charged or read her rights; she just would not remember. Her long-term memory was fine; it was easy for her to hide her dark secrets. Two weeks before the case, Sarah went to see her and told her what was happening and told her that she was just as guilty. She had told Mum that David had gone to the police, and my mother's words were, "Well he always was a troublemaker." Sarah was shocked at this and refused to visit her until after the trial. "I'm going to tell her the outcome. I can't wait," she said.

"When I left home at 16, I vowed never to see her again, I will not come with you when you tell her. I really can't look her in the face without being totally disgusted at what I see, she was never a mother to me." None of us got any sleep that night; going through both of our minds were the questions we could be asked and what ifs. The alarm went off at 6 am; she was already downstairs and had been since 4 am. She looked so stressed and exhausted, I tried to lighten the mood but I wasn't feeling much better than her. "Sarah," I said, "I know this is really tough but we are doing the right thing." "I know," she replied.

## The Case
Trial Day 2

In the following order we were supposed to give our evidence: David on Monday, along with his ex-wife and daughter, on Tuesday I was supposed to go first, then Tom followed by Sarah and her ex-husband in the afternoon. Tom picked us up at eight o' clock as promised, looking very smart. I took one look at him and remembered this was the man I fell for all those years ago, this is the man standing with me through all of this, and he did look so good. We arrived at the court very early so we decided to find somewhere for a cup of tea; a small coffee shop was just opening in the marketplace. It was a bitterly cold morning, and I was wrapped up in a white wool coat and a heavy scarf around my neck. Tom held my hand and wouldn't let go. "I am so proud of you," he said. "This is so brave." Time was pressing on so we made our way to the court; there seemed to be a lot of people going in and out, but I didn't feel nervous at that point. As we went through the scanning machines one by one, first Sarah, then me, suddenly the scanner went *bleep bleep*. The security guard looked at me. "Oh." He then pulled out his hand scanner and waved it over my shoulder and again the bleep confirmed it. I was then allowed through. A plate in my shoulder set it off, and I have the same at airports and sometimes shop scanners. We collected our belongings from the trays and continued to the foyer. Lin and her colleague were waiting with Sarah and her counsellor. We were greeted with warm smiles and hugs. Hillery remarked, "I don't think you should stand here too long, as your dad may walk through the doors at any moment." I really needed the ladies' and said to Tom, "Wait here I won't be long." Just to the left of the foyer I spotted the ladies' toilets. As I came out my blood ran cold: Dad was heading for the gents' just next door; we came face to face. There was no reaction from him, just a cold blank stare. That stare sent shivers down my spine. He didn't have to speak, I knew what he was thinking; the threats he had made to me sprang straight to the front of my head. "I will kill you," I expected him to say there and then. I quickly looked away to see Hillery running toward me. "I tried to get to you first to warn you," she said, "but I didn't make it in time." My face was red and my heart was pounding as if trying to jump out of my chest; I was shaking with fear. "We had better go straight through to the witness protection area now," said Lin. "You will be safer there, he can't get to you there." We rejoined everyone and moved swiftly down a corridor to the witness area. "I saw him," Sarah announced. "I saw him but I was so scared I hid behind a pillar." She too was physically shaking.

Tom held my hand so tight and tried to comfort me. I tried to hold back the tears. "It's okay," he said, "he's gone now, he's gone. Don't worry I won't let him hurt you." The witness area was made up of small rooms with glass partition walls and a round table in the middle. There were a few chairs but not enough for all of us. Lin collected a few from the empty room and placed them around the table; aside from us there was a huge screen that gave information about the courts and names of people due to appear in court and times. "I will get us a cup of tea," said Lin. "Make that a bucket!" I piped up. "And a few valium as well!" That raised a chuckle amongst everyone; it did make me feel slightly better. I don't know where my weird humor comes from in time of crisis, but it seems to help me through.

Tom found the big screen fascinating. "Your dad's not on there yet so we are okay for a minute." That didn't help my terrified look, as I knew I would be called first to give evidence. I was fast losing faith in my own words "we can do this"; now I wasn't so sure. Lin handed me a tea in a disposable cup. I remember thinking, I'm going to need a lot more tea than that.

It didn't seem right that David was not here. I asked Lin what had happened the day before. She explained that he had given his evidence, but he was so distressed he didn't want to talk and went straight home. I asked, "Did you manage to tell him that we are also giving evidence?" "Yes," she said, "I told him but he just wanted to get out of here, he was very upset." I understood his actions, and even though we had not spoken for so many years, I still wanted to do the right thing by him. If he decided he didn't want to speak to me or Sarah I accepted his wishes, and also understood his loneliness and his isolation and his mistrust of everyone. Lin, Hillery, and Dee sat and made light conversation about the weather.

A court usher appeared and explained the rules and procedures to us. We were not allowed to discuss the case here or anywhere until everyone had given their evidence. We were told that the courtroom we would be giving our evidence in was court seven. As she was talking I kept looking at my watch; she talked for around 20 minutes and then left. It was now getting on for quarter to ten. By this time I had drank four cups of the weak tea and was ready for a refill. Tom offered to get yet another, and as he returned with the tea so did the usher (Elizabeth, she said). This is it. I began to take really deep breaths as I left my seat. "You can do it," he said as he placed the tea on a small table. I kept telling myself "deep breaths, deep breaths." Everyone wished me luck and said, "It will soon be over, you can do it." My counsellor Dee, the court usher, and I left the room and headed towards court seven.

The corridors were very long and it seemed to take ages to get to the courtroom. All three of us stood outside the courtroom,

## THE CASE AND THE TRIAL

the huge wooden doors firmly shut. While I was still taking deep breaths, Dee turned to me and said, "You will be okay, trust me you will do fine." The big wooden doors opened and I entered the court. I did not look to my left at the public gallery but made my way into the witness box. I could barely see over the top of it, and there was a small microphone to the left of me. I then noticed a blue screen shielding me from view. I began to panic. I didn't ask for the screen to be in place, I did not want to be shielded from view—I wanted the whole room to see I was telling the truth. Suddenly I said, get ahold of yourself, you're here now so get on with it. The room was huge, and the jury seemed to be quite a distance away; I tried to make out their faces but couldn't.

Two weeks before the trail began, I was asked by the police if I wanted to be shielded from the public gallery and my father. I had said no, but I did ask if I could have a chair; just as well they didn't give me one that day as I wouldn't have been seen at all. Swearing on the Bible first, then the judge asked if I could move the microphone closer to me so I could be heard. The barrister for the prosecution spoke (Mr. Talor) the questions; he asked me about our house and things that Dad and Mum had done. His questions lasted about half an hour, each question delivered with care and appreciation for my very fragile state. Then came the defense. I had already asked for two glasses of water; I needed another before I was verbally attacked by my dad's barrister. The judge asked if I was okay as the tears flowed down my cheeks, once again reliving the nightmares of my childhood. "Do you want to continue?" he asked. "Yes," I replied. I wanted this over. Dad's defense stood and began his cross-examination. I knew this would be unbearable but I had to do it, I had to go on. Aiming all of my answers at the jury, I continued. Dad's barrister spoke: "I put it to you that you have collaborated this story along with your brother and sister to blacken your father's name, and also for financial gain. You aim to take all of his money." I firmly said this was not true; how could this be true as I have not spoken to my brother for over 22 years? He went on to say that Dad had a phone call from a woman who told him that his daughters would screw him for every penny. "I put it to you," he said, "you made this phone call to your father." I firmly said I did not and again faced the jury. He then said, "I have no doubt that your story is a complete fabrication." I was asked to explain what Dad had done to me over and over. The questions put to me had the same answers. "Yes my father raped me, yes he made me do things, yes this is all true," I sobbed. MR Mortimer continued, "Did you tell anyone? Why didn't you tell your mother?"

I was beginning to think this man must be so stupid. Did he not listen to me? "Mother was involved, she is a pedophile too, she encouraged all of it." At this he looked at the judge and said, "I have no further questions, Your Honor." I was very irritated by this. I wanted to tell him more, I felt robbed. As I opened my mouth to speak, the judge said, "You may leave the witness box, you are free to go." Still in a state of shock, I left the box and courtroom. Dee followed me out. "God," she said, "you were amazing." Mr. Taylor said, "If

## THE CASE AND THE TRIAL

all witnesses were like you we would win every case. Wow, totally amazing." We walked back to the witness protection area. I was still feeling I had not been allowed to say enough. I blurted out to Tom how I felt, and how I'd wanted to say more but was stopped in my tracks by the defense. "Do you know you have been gone an hour and a half? I have been pacing the floor and Hillery has been trying to keep me still. I'm so proud of you."

I looked at Sarah. "You can do this, it's okay, you will be okay." Tom was up next. As he disappeared with the court usher, the questions I had been asked and the answers I had given were buzzing like bees in my head. He was back within half an hour. I couldn't ask him what went on and how he was questioned; we were told not to discuss what went on. God I wanted to know what he was asked and how he'd replied. When he returned, he also looked drained and a bit confused. Sarah was called next; I could see she was completely terrified. Hillery, Sarah, and the usher made their way to the courtroom. As she passed, I hugged her and said she will be okay, I am here waiting you will be fine; she forced a smile. There were three cups of tea lined up on the table, one for Tom and two for me. It was over, I had done it; it felt so good to get this all out. I had told a room full of complete strangers about Dad and Mum; and most of all, Dad had to listen to every word of it. I secretly said a little prayer for Sarah as I sipped my tea. After an hour she appeared with Hillery; she was in floods of tears. Hillery tried to console her; I couldn't speak to her. She was taken to a side room out of the way. I wanted to throw my arms around her and tell her she was so brave. I was not allowed for fear we might discuss the case and jeopardize the whole thing. The court had adjourned for lunch. Tom and I went outside to get some air and stretch our legs; we then returned to the witness area ready for the afternoon. Sarah had only been questioned that morning by the prosecution and had to go back into the courtroom to be cross-examined. In an hour a remarkable transformation emerged: she was smiling and looked up at me and said, "I am ready now, bring it on." I was amazed. From somewhere she had gained the strength to go on; like a butterfly emerging from a chrysalis, she was more herself now than she had ever been. Her name was called again, and she along with Hillery returned to the courtroom. I was surprised when she returned from the room half an hour later still smiling. "It's over now," she said. "I have done it, I have told everyone about that bastard, it's over." Everyone clapped and cheered, "Well done, well done." Her ex-husband was called as a witness next; to our surprise he was in and out in ten minutes. There were other witnesses that the judge decided would not be required, and the day finished around four thirty.

I had never seen my sister so happy and was truly amazed at the difference in her.

## Day 3

Things were moving on so quickly; even the police hadn't seen a case like this move on so fast. Day three was summing-up

## THE CASE AND THE TRIAL

day. Dee and Hillery suggested it would be best not to sit through this, and tried to persuade Sarah it would upset her if she sat in the public gallery and listened to all of it.

Tom, however, sat through the whole thing.

Sarah filled that day with a spot of shopping, dragging me along in and out the stores in town. I wasn't a bit interested in shopping. I wanted so much to be a fly on the wall in that courtroom, wondering what was being said about me, Sarah, and David.

After she got all her goodies from the stores, we jumped on the bus and went back to hers.

I couldn't think straight all afternoon and desperately waited for Tom to call.

I tried to settle and read a book, but my mind kept drifting back to that courtroom.

At around five the phone rang.

"Hi," Tom said. "What a day, I have listened and heard things that reduced me to tears, you were wise not to be there today, it was best.

"I've heard so much my head is buzzing.

"Do you want me to come over?

"If you don't want me to that's okay, you say."

"We need to talk," I replied.

Pacing the floor now at Sarah's, I couldn't wait for him to turn up; for the first time I wanted to run away from all of this.

Sarah was busy in the kitchen. I didn't want to be here right now; I needed some space away from her as well.

Tom arrived about seven. I grabbed my shoes and yelled out to her, "I'll see you later."

That night we talked and talked. Tom sobbed and I sobbed.

"How can you ever forgive me? I am so very sorry."

He went on to say about the summing up and how the defense had called us liars, but the judge told the jury to disregard this and Mr. Mortimer was firmly told not to slander us as we were not there to defend ourselves.

Tom went on to say that the defense suggested we had made it all up because we were after Dad's money.

When asked by the prosecution whether Dad had money or property or any assets, Dad said no.

My dad was living in a sheltered accommodation.

"Then the prosecution looked at me and asked the jury to look at me also.

"'You see the well-dressed gentleman at the back, does he look like he needs a pensioner's money?'"

Tom sobbed again. "I've heard things today that have had a

huge effect on my life.

"I do understand now, everything is clear to me.

"You are my life, I have been so stupid, forgive me, please forgive me."

"Please take me back to Sarah," I said. "We will talk more soon, maybe we can try to repair some of the damage to our marriage, maybe there is hope for us."

## Day 4

The summing up spilled over to day four of the trial; back at the witness protection area we sat and talked.

We are all told to be hopeful for a verdict that day.

The time presses on and the jury is out.

Both Tom and I are pacing up and down, sitting, standing, going outside for a cigarette, more pacing. The pressure so intense.

Each time we returned from outside, hoping there would be some news.

Then lunch, still no news; we all left to grab a bite to eat. This time we all sat together and did nothing else but talk about the case, as we had all given our evidence.

I don't know how, but Tom found out that Dad's barrister strongly advised him to plead guilty in the hope he would get a lesser sentence. "That's not his way," I said.

## BEHIND BARS

We returned to the court after lunch. The security at the court got quite used to me bleeping as I went through the body scanner; the metal plate in my shoulder set it off every time.

As soon as we sat, Lin appeared. She looked tense.

The jury had verdicts on 19 of the 23 charges, but we still didn't know if these were guilty or not guilty. The charges against Dad were being whittled down for the case from seventy-two to twenty-three in order for the Crown Prosecution Service to proceed with a prosecution.

The atmosphere was really tense; more pacing, more tea, even more cigarettes.

Time moved so slowly; now approaching 4 pm and still nothing.

Even Lin, Hillery, and Dee looked exhausted.

The jury had been out all day and no verdict.

Tom tried to keep spirits up, saying, "That's usually a good sign." I just couldn't find it in me to believe him.

I feared the worst. We had been through so much, and it would all be for nothing if he was found not guilty. Those words echoed in my head all night long.

When dressing the following morning, getting ready for day five, we both wore odd socks hoping it might bring us luck.

Looking down at her socks, she remarked, "Well, they didn't

work yesterday when we put them on, did they?" My heart felt as heavy as hers.

"No, they haven't worked yet." Not quite believing my own words.

"We will try again today."

That morning I had one orange sock and one blue sock, and Sarah the same.

"Don't give up yet, it's nearly over, they will work today you will see."

## Day 5

We didn't tell anyone about our crazy socks, and to be honest the stress of the morning made me forget I was wearing them.

On Thursday Libby, one of the other police officers involved in the case, said she would pop into the court; it was her day off but she was not going to miss the verdict for anything.

This time Sarah and I got the bus to the court and arranged to meet Tom, Hillery, and Dee outside.

It was bitterly cold. We made our way to the witness area again.

Lin was already inside. As we sat, Tom monitored the screens whilst making a tea.

"I think this will all be over very soon and a verdict will be here before 10," said Dee.

Lin piped up, "No, I think 11.30." Tom said 12. Sarah said 12.30 and I said 12.45.

Libby popped in as promised. "Have I missed anything?" "No, not yet," said Hillery, "not yet."

By 11 still no verdict. A call came over the tannoy, "Would all parties in the Stear trial please return to the courtroom."

My hands went up to my mouth. This must be it—my heart almost jumping out of my chest.

"He's been found not guilty, I know it." Sarah was getting so upset, she started crying.

Tom tried to tell her not to worry but it wasn't working.

Lin went to the courtroom but was back within five minutes.

The jury wanted to verify one question.

Was that it? Still no verdict. My heart felt like it had been ripped from my chest and thrown down a pit, then stamped on.

12 o'clock came and went; so did 12.30 and still no verdict.

I tried so hard to keep Sarah's spirits up but it was near impossible; by this time the tension was at breaking point. I grabbed Tom's arm and said I needed to get some air.

He was trying to stay positive; by this time the pressure was getting to him too. We went outside for a cigarette.

# THE CASE AND THE TRIAL

"Come on," he said, "we had better go back in."

As we walked back to the room, Lin was standing and it looked like she had something to say.

"We have a verdict." Her face still gave nothing away; my hands went up to cover my mouth. The silence before she spoke again was sheer agony.

Then she announced quite calmly, "GUILTY."

I was ecstatic, Sarah had her hands on her cheeks; Tom, Libby, and Lin all hugged.

I hugged Sarah. "It's over now, it's over.

"What about David? Have you told him?"

Lin said, "I was in that courtroom, my heart was pounding, and all of this didn't happen to me but I had palpitations and then came the rest of the charges.

"Guilty, guilty, guilty, guilty, guilty, guilty, guilty, guilty, guilty, guilty, guilty. Guilty, guilty, guilty, guilty, guilty, guilty, guilty, guilty, guilty, guilty, guilty."

I couldn't believe my ears; by this time, the room had erupted in cheers and tears of relief.

It's finally over, it's finally over, now I can begin to live my life; you, my father, you will affect me no more. It's done.

That small room was bursting with energy and emotion.

Lin asked if we wanted to speak to the press.

There had been press interest from day one of the trial; it seemed they were keen to talk to us.

This story was groundbreaking stuff, as never before had such a historic case won with such a strong guilty verdict.

A reporter from the *Evening Post* had sat through the case all week.

On the first day, when David gave his evidence, he returned to his office and handed it to his editor. He was stopped in his tracks and the article was spiked; his editor referred to it as being too horrific to print.

Lin moved herself away from all of the noise to make a call to David; she seemed a bit tense, she had good news and bad news to give him. "Hello," she said. I could tell she was talking to him and when she said the word "guilty" to him, she had to move the phone away from her ear as David was also ecstatic, his excitement was so loud. She allowed the din to die down before she spoke again. "David, that's not all. I have to tell you that the jury is still out on one count, and that is the one against you, the verdict is still undecided." I couldn't believe it. He brought the case to court, he stood up and gave his evidence; I don't understand how the jury could not decide whether he was telling the truth. All went quiet at the end of the phone; I was shocked and saddened for my brother. Lin finished her call and returned to the still excited crowd. She explained that the final charge will probably come

## THE CASE AND THE TRIAL

back not guilty. As those words left her lips, she was called to return to the courtroom. A look of sadness still on her face, she said, "I feel as if I have let your brother down." Within five minutes she returned with a huge grin on her face. "Oh it's so nice to be wrong sometimes," she said. She flung her arms in the air and said, "Guilty on all accounts." The jury was asked to go with a majority verdict. The emotion in the room was overwhelming. Lin pulled out her phone once more to call David. I could hear him scream with delight. I was so stunned at the verdict.

All through the case Dad had maintained he was innocent; he had lied to everyone, he had lied in the courtroom. Dad asked to be sentenced that same day, but the judge said he would not sentence him as he requested—the case was too severe and even he would have to seek guidance before sentencing. Dad was taken down and there he will remain for the rest of his days.

Ironic how the table turns: we were vulnerable children and he is now a vulnerable pensioner. I have my justice and my life begins now. This is the last day of his freedom, but the very first day of ours. Mr. Taylor joined us in the witness area still wearing his wig and robe; he shook my hand and said I was a brilliant witness. "Your father will be looking at a hefty sentence, it may be six or seven years, he will probably die in prison." He sat for a while between Sarah and me and placed his wig on the table. "Thank you so much, Mr. Taylor, for all you have done, you have helped to change our lives."

◄ BEHIND BARS

"Well, Sis? Haven't you forgotten about something, haven't you forgotten about our lucky charm?" She smiled and at the same time we displayed our odd socks. Mr. Taylor found this very amusing and the girls did too.

CHAPTER **21**

# The Press

"I hope you don't mind," said Mr. Taylor, "but the press are outside and are keen to talk to you both.

"My wife also would like to talk to you first."

I looked at Sarah. I knew we would have to face this but unlike the fear that filled me before, somehow I was ready to face them.

However, I was wondering why the barrister's wife would want to talk to us.

We both agreed to speak to the press and to speak with Mrs. Taylor.

During the case, we had discussed the possibility that this story would hit the press and how we would react, both of us not looking forward to the exposure of our story and how it would affect our families. But strangely, our outlook had changed and the prospect of telling our story became so important to us.

## BEHIND BARS

How many people, I wondered, had also been affected by Dad; after all, in later years he became a ballroom dance teacher.

Could it be that many others suffered too?

In his job he would have had contact with children.

This made telling our story inevitable. "I want to reach out and tell the world," said Sarah.

Dee and Hillery both mentioned that in other cases like ours, people rarely spoke to the press.

I wondered whether the thought had crossed my brother's mind.

Oh how I wanted to talk to him.

I wanted so much to throw my arms around him and thank him from the bottom of my heart.

It would be amazing for us all to be together.

When Lin was on the phone to him an hour ago, I wanted to take the phone from her and tell him he was my hero, he had the guts to make that call to the police, he started the ball rolling. What courage—"thank you" just was not enough.

As Mr. Taylor left the witness area, a man in a dark suit appeared.

"Hello," he said. "I know this is probably not the right time to talk, I will respect your wishes if you want me to go away."

Sarah looked at me; I think she wanted me to speak first.

My name is Clive Bolton, I'm a reporter at the *Evening Post*.

He held out his hand. I shook it and so did Sarah. I couldn't help but notice his shirt was rather dirty. "I wondered," he said, "if you were up to making a small statement?

"I've been at the court all week following your story; do you think your brother would be willing to talk to me?"

I replied, "I don't have an answer to that." He went on to say he wanted to be as sensitive as possible with whatever was published.

To my surprise Sarah piped up, "Yes we will give you a statement, and I want you to put our names in the paper."

"You do realise that you will waive your right to anonymity if you do this?" "Yes, she said, "that's okay.

"I'm sure Elizabeth feels the way I do.

"We want to name and shame that bastard, and our mother too.

"So far she has got away with all of this, we both feel it's the right thing to do."

We had a strong feeling that even more family members had been affected by Dad.

My dad's brother Phil went to prison for five years for abusing his children; my cousin Arthur was at court with us the whole week. He knew things about Dad that we didn't.

Some of the things he mentioned, though, did bring back painful memories.

Sarah was also abused by another of Dad's brothers.

Yes we had a very good reason to speak to the press; if we can help one person by telling our story, it would all be worth it.

Our aim, by telling our story, was very clear.

We sat for about fifteen minutes and Clive made a few notes. He asked questions such as how do we feel now that our ordeal is finally over, and also about our childhood, being very careful not to upset both of us.

"I have the background to the case and this will go in tomorrow's edition." He then thanked us both and then left.

We were about to leave and head outside to the foyer when Mr. Taylor came over and introduced a tall blonde lady that stood with him.

"This is my wife," he said. "I hope you don't mind but can you spare her five minutes?"

"Oh I am sorry. I had forgotten, yes you wanted to talk to us, didn't you?"

The blonde lady held out her hand. "My name is Rebecca, I've been living with your case all week," she said. "You," she said, "must be Elizabeth." She was looking directly at Sarah.

"No, I am Elizabeth." "Oh I'm so sorry, I knew I would get it wrong." She giggled nervously.

"The reason I asked my husband if I could speak with you, well I am not just his wife, I am also a freelance journalist."

"Well talk about the ideal job, right there in the courtroom, with all the stories you hear, that must be perfect for you." I didn't mean to sound sarcastic, but anyway she took it well.

I bet it was a match made in heaven, I thought.

"I write articles for some of the top magazines and would love to do a spread on this case; how do you feel about that? I will understand if you say no as this is so sensitive a case and my intention is not to upset you.

"You have all been through so much, I can assure you I will be very careful not to offend you or cause you any distress.

"You have all been amazing and so brave."

She must be reading my mind, I thought, as she went on to say, "I am sure your story will help other people that may be suffering the effects of abuse to speak out and come forward."

Sarah looked at me; this time she wanted me to speak first.

Without hesitation, I agreed that anything to bring this to the public's attention and let them know that no matter how old the history of abuse is, people can still be prosecuted for their sickening offenses.

People like my father. I know there are many more out there like him.

No more will it be brushed under the carpet; no more will it be tolerated.

When in the sixties and seventies, you just were not believed if you spoke out.

I have a cousin who when she was eight was put into a home because she was, so they say , a difficult child. I would dearly love to know the truth.

I have never believed that story; one day the truth will come out.

Rebecca was keen to get her story there and then, but both Sarah and I were exhausted and just wanted to go home; we arranged to meet her on Sunday.

She gave us both her card and we said good-bye.

I couldn't stop thinking about David. Rebecca said she was about to call him before we left. I asked, "Please can you tell him we are thinking about him?" and handed her my home number.

Arthur was waiting outside with Tom; he wanted to be here to give us the support.

His dad at least put his hand up and admitted he was guilty, unlike my dad, who throughout maintained he was innocent.

What a total bastard and a coward.

Arthur was ecstatic. "You got him then, you did it. Well done. I'm so pleased for you."

He flung his arms around both of us and the tears began to flow.

Arthur too had been traumatized by his abusive childhood, and now in his early fifties was overwhelmed at the outcome of our trial.

"I must go and call my wife, how good this is and that you got justice for what that bastard did.

"It's great, it's so great. I will call you to find out the date of the sentencing. I wouldn't miss it for the world, see you all soon."

He was still punching the air when he walked away.

Sarah, Tom, and I got the bus back to her house; flashing through my head, a picture of Lin saying, "We have a verdict."

I didn't speak for the whole journey, I was just so tired; this week had seemed so long, and the thought of going back to work tomorrow filled me with panic.

"Are you okay?" Tom asked, looking concerned. "Yes, I just don't feel like talking," still trying to take in everything that had happened that day and the whole week.

We arrived at Sarah's. I announced I was going straight back home, gathering up my things as quickly as I could. My youngest said his good-byes to her boys. Turning to Sarah and saying, "I will give you a call when I get home, okay?"

As we got into the car, I asked him not to speak all of the way home.

He nodded and said, "Okay, Mum."

During my drive home I began thinking about Tom too; he stuck by me, he had heard everything.

I have seen my husband cry real tears for me.

He still wants me and says he loves me more than ever. I never believed him, I shut him out.

I have seen a different man.

I love him too, but I don't know how to express this to him.

*Love* is a strange word to me. I have to learn to love like a child learns to walk and talk.

I hope I can do this.

Maybe this is a second chance for us. Can we put all of this behind us and make our marriage work? Deep down, I knew this was what we both wanted.

The man I've always wanted was already there.

We arrived home at around eight that evening. "Leave the bags in the car, I will get them in the morning before I go

# THE PRESS

to work." Due to start work that Saturday at eleven am, a prospect I was really not looking forward to.

That evening, for the first time I slept soundly. I was on a later start tomorrow and would be finished by eight. I left for work well in time for a tea before my shift started. As I gathered aprons from my locker at work, one of the girls from the counters tapped me on the shoulder. "How did it go?" I turned and just burst into floods of tears and collapsed onto the floor.

The outpouring had begun; Dee had warned me this would happen.

The aftermath, the total exhaustion and relief that it was all over. I realised then I should go home; I was in no fit state to be at work.

She didn't know what to say. "I'm going home," I said. "I can't cope with work today."

Leaving work, I went home and back to bed.

The phone was ringing; it woke me. "Please answer it." I heard my youngest talking and then he hung up.

Drowsy from my sleep, I asked, "Who was that on the phone?"

I hadn't realised that I had slept that long; it was now seven in the evening.

I jumped out of bed. "Mum, the call was from a man." "Who?" I asked. "I don't know, he said he will call back."

# BEHIND BARS

Teenage boys make lousy secretaries, I thought.

Sitting with my cup of tea in the conservatory, I was deep in thought. Where do we go from here? Often I sat in darkness.

For the past year leading up to the trial, I had broken down several times at work; it was so hard to keep going. My boss didn't understand until one day WHAM—my face appeared all over most of the papers. The press did not exaggerate any of my story. The girls at work were so pleased to see me and asked how the case had gone.

I handed them a newspaper each and said, "Read it for yourself. We won." Bursting into tears again.

CHAPTER **22**

# David

David had also spoken to the press, but his statements were collected separately from ours.

Through the whole case we had not spoken and our paths never crossed.

Rebecca promised me she would pass on my home number, although my heart sank as I had to accept he didn't want to speak to Sarah or me.

Busy in the kitchen preparing tea that evening, the phone rang. I was getting a bit annoyed, as since the press release, the phone was constantly ringing.

Agents wanting more of a story.

"Don't answer that," I yelled from the kitchen, but I was too late. Studying my son's face to try and make out who was calling.

"Oh Mum, it's for you, someone called David."

## BEHIND BARS

Mixed emotions and shock took over; I dropped the loaf of bread in my hand.

"David, oh my God. Grabbing the phone from his hand, a voice at the other end said, "Hello, Sis."

The tears started to flow once more. "Oh David, I'm so pleased you rang. I can't thank you enough, you have changed my life, how can I put into words what you have done for me? You are a wonderful brother, just amazing. I owe you everything.

"You are so brave, so brave to make that call."

I couldn't stop blubbering.

We talked and talked for over an hour. It was truly fantastic. After all these years, I have my brother back. We said our good-byes, and I promised to meet up with him at Sarah's house the following Sunday.

It was amazing to talk to my brother and the rest of the evening I was so excited, trying to picture what my own brother looked like.

Also excited about the chance to meet my niece; the last time I saw her she was a tiny baby.

Now a fully grown woman—wow, it was so much to take in.

Can't help thinking that Dad was responsible for driving such a wedge between us all.

## DAVID

This was about to change for good: we, all three of us, will be together under one roof next Sunday.

I couldn't wait.

The days dragged at work.

"I don't know what has happened to you," said Sheila, "you seem such a different person. I know you have been through so much, but the way you are now is amazing, full of life, full of energy."

"Put it like this," I said.

"It feels like the weight of a thousand tons has been lifted from my shoulders.

"The truth really has set me free, the past is done, the future for me starts now.

"I am free of the guilt, the shame, and depression, free from the trauma of my past.

"My second chance is here and I'm sure going to make the most of it.

"No one is going to stop me now, living my life to the full.

"I feel I deserve it," and with a huge grin said, "I'm sure worth it." Sheila chuckled. David called me last night and we talked for ages; it was so wonderful to hear his voice.

## BEHIND BARS

Sheila smiled and threw her arms around me; she had tears in her eyes too.

The happy ending.

Oh what a happy ending.

Some of the girls at work read the four-page article in the chat magazine and all of the papers that ran the story.

A couple of the girls found it very difficult to read.

One of the girls said, "These things happen to people far away, to people you don't know, not your friends."

When I returned to work after the case, I gave my boss a copy of the magazine. "You need to read this," I said.

"I don't know whether I want to," was her reply.

"Take it home with you and read it, this may help you to understand what I had to go through with very little support."

I was angry with her for her attitude toward me during my difficult year.

"Going without pay to attend court, and I was the butt of some cruel jokes here, life could have been made a little easier for me but you didn't seem to care."

She accepted the magazine and promised to return it the following day.

One copy I carefully placed on the centre table in the canteen for all of the staff to read if they wished.

I wanted to send a double-barreled message to them all.

Attaching a little note to it simply saying,

*It's never too late.*

The message was loud and clear for anyone affected by a similar past to know that they can still get the help and the closure that I have.

Even after forty years.

The second message: anyone who has committed such awful crimes of abuse with children will be found out, sooner or later.

People whispered behind my back whenever I entered the canteen, staring and poking one another.

Treating me like a leper.

Three members of the staff came to me and broke the icy feel. "How brave of you, what a nightmare you have been through, thankfully you can put it behind you now."

My boss returned the magazine the following day.

"When you told me about all of this, I thought it was just your brother, you didn't say it was you as well, I'm so sorry, I didn't understand."

## BEHIND BARS

The store manager decided it would be best to remove the magazine and all of the newspapers containing our story—which was pretty much every newspaper—from the canteen, and the magazines from the store.

How narrow-minded of them. They couldn't see the bigger picture, the message in the story.

At home the phone rang every five minutes or so: different press agencies wanting a piece of the action.

We declined most of them, just wanting now to concentrate on our own healing.

Getting to know the real person in my brother and sister.

Knowing and feeling their pain too, understanding their ways.


Driving to my sister's house early that Sunday morning, I was feeling so nervous, trying to picture my brother's face and how he would react to me after all these years.

Not forgetting his daughter, trying to picture a young lady's face.

My youngest asked lots of questions on the journey, some I didn't have the answers to.

We arrived at Sarah's around nine thirty; she put a cup of tea straight into my hand and hugged me so tight.

A huge grin spread across her face. "I feel fantastic," she said, and her smile got even wider.

My heart started to pound. "I'm so nervous." "So am I," she said, "but I'm excited too."

The boys disappeared as usual and left me and Sarah to talk.

Then a knock at the door. "It's David," she said; my hands were getting so sweaty with nerves.

I need not have worried so much. David popped his head around the door, a huge grin on his face.

"Hello, Sis," he said, "you've still got your looks then."

He hugged me so tight, and his tears began to flow.

"This is wonderful, so wonderful," he sobbed.

"We are together, I had to do it, I had to stop that bastard and I'm so glad I did.

I've got my sisters back." He sobbed and sobbed; he grabbed my hand and didn't let go.

Then a little blonde head popped around the door. "Hello, Auntie Liz." "Oh my God, it's little Lisa."

I hugged her and David together; it was such a wonderful day and one I will never forget.

Such a precious day; all four of us clung to each other for ages, and so much to talk about.

We talked about the day of the sentencing and how we all need to be together, united.

David was not sure if he wanted to go back to court. I assured him we would be together throughout and it was what he needed to see. The end to his torture, the end to his nightmares.

As I left Sarah's, I promised to keep in touch often and was hoping David would change his mind.

We needed to stand together for this.

I did understand his pain, but his role in all of this was not quite finished yet. "Don't you want to see Dad go down?" I asked him.

"Don't you want to hear what the judge will say?

"You, my brave brother, so brave to come forward and make that call and go through all of this.

"You've got to see it to the end."

He held my hand before I left and said he would think about it.

"We must stand together again," said Sarah. "Please come with us and get your justice."

As we left Sarah's at the same time, David honked his horn several times.

Sarah turned to me. "I hope he does come to the sentencing,

## DAVID

the final hurdle, I know it will help all of us if we are there together."

Saying good-bye to her and her boys, I made my way back home.

Sleep didn't come easy that night, being still in a state of excitement.

What a wonderful day we all had. My youngest talked for hours with his newfound cousin, getting on so well together.

I had never seen my brother and my sister so ecstatically happy, and it certainly was contagious. I'm sure I was still grinning when I finally dozed off.

The phone was ringing off the hook; it woke me up.

"Hello, hi Sis, it's me." "Hi, David." "I have decided, after thinking about it all night, I will be at the sentencing, I will see that bastard taken down once and for all.

"We will see him go down together. It's what we all need to do."

CHAPTER **23**

# The Sentencing

We talked and talked for another hour. "I've got something for you and Sarah," he said. "I will bring it to the court, it's for both of you to keep. I'm not going to tell you what it is, as it is a surprise, but I know you will like it." Being very curious as to what his surprise might be, we said our goodbyes. "Love you, Sis," he said as he put down the phone.

The reporter from the *Evening Post* rang the following day with a date from the sentencing, then shortly after a call from the police; the date was set for the 7th of December. It was a bitterly cold morning when we arrived at court. Again we were taken to the witness area. It seemed we had been there so many times before, knowing the way through the labyrinth of corridors and all so familiar.

Only a few weeks earlier we had paced up and down in a frantic state under such terrible stress; this time, everything was so different. This time this building was a friend. There was no sign of David. Getting a bit concerned, I turned to

## THE SENTENCING

Sarah. "Where is he? I do hope he is still coming." The court usher appeared and began to explain the procedure and how we would be called to the courtroom. The party for the prosecution will all go in together. This was the moment I was truly waiting for; once this is out of the way there will be no stopping my confidence. I am me, this is it—the final hurdle.

I gazed down at my watch; time was going so slowly and still no sign of David. Then he arrived looking very windswept and clutching a carrier bag under his arm; we hugged. The girls, Dee, Hillery, Lin, and Libby, were all close to tears as they knew we had not seen one another for so many years. "Well what an ending to all of this," said Dee. "This is so lovely to see." Tom piped up, "I'm a great believer in the saying, 'Out of every seed of adversity, comes a seed of equal or greater benefit.'" This was so true of us three. David placed the bag on the table and pulled out three photo frames. Inside the frame, a poem set amongst three lamps; he gave one to Sarah and one to me.

"This sums up everything for me," he said. "I really hope you like it. The words describe all three of us and the lamps are three."

David placed the third on the table for the girls to read. After reading the poem, the girls reached for their hankies. "That's so lovely and so true, David," I said. "This is us. No other words can describe us like this, I will treasure it for the rest of my days."

## BEHIND BARS

Three warm flames from the darkness rise
Shines alight on shattered lives
The spread of the light and the warmth of three candles blaze
I now look forward to the salvaged love from forgotten days.

United we are strong although divided we never fell
So with conscience if you have any?
Take this to your resting place

Rising from the ashes
Us three finally found our grace.

David 25/11/2010

This beautiful poem hangs on my wall and I read it daily. I thank my brother from the bottom of my heart; when I'm feeling low the words pick me straight up again.

Sarah had mentioned a call from Arthur the night before.

Five years previously, Arthur had stood in the very same witness box giving evidence against his father, my dad's brother, for abusing him and his sisters too.

I remember at my grandmother's funeral in full view of Dad's brothers and sisters, even his sister, my aunt from Australia, we witnessed Phil handcuffed and escorted by two prison officers.

Arthur was thrilled that we also had a guilty verdict and asked, "Can I come along for the sentencing?" "I'm sure it will be okay," she said.

"I want to see that bastard go down too," he said.

"I knew he was doing things to you all just like Dad did to me, and I can't wait to see you all tomorrow, thanks."

That morning Arthur joined us in the witness area.

He hugged us all with tears in his eyes.

"You did it, the three of you. You did it," he said, "well done to you, it takes a lot of guts, it was really tough for me too, so I know what you have all been through, well done to you, well done."

Wiping his eyes, he picked up the photo frame and read the poem. "This is brilliant," he said. "Can I have a copy?"

David agreed to make a copy for him.

We were all so busy talking; the small room was full.

The court usher appeared and got quite lost between us all.

She cleared her throat and announced, "The Crown versus Mr. Stear, please make your way to the courtroom."

This was it, Dad was about to find out his fate. "Thank you and please follow me." The room fell silent in seconds. We all made our way to the corridor and the first available lift; it was quite a squeeze getting us all in. As we approached the courtroom, David grabbed my hand so tight that my fingers began to go blue. This time I did turn to look in the public gallery. Two older ladies looked in our direction and then put their heads together as if whispering about us. We took seats at the front stalls. David began to shake, holding my hand even tighter. A woman to my left leaned into me. "In case you are wondering, I'm a police officer and I'm waiting for another case to start in this courtroom." That's a bit odd, I thought, but just left it at that. Behind me and towards the middle of the room, the empty dock.

Sarah and David kept their eyes firmly forward; the judge entered and sat ready to commence with the proceedings.

He then spoke to our barrister.

"Am I right in thinking that the minimum sentence for rape of a minor is ten years?

"Am I also right in thinking that this also constitutes a gross indecency, which in itself carries a sentence of two years?"

To both questions our barrister, Mr. Taylor, replied,

"Yes, my lord."

The doors behind the dock opened. Dad was escorted by two prison guards; as they entered, I took a good look at him. That same cold face stared at me. I turned.

Now fixing my eyes firmly on the judge's face.

Mr. Taylor stood, then delivered his speech.

Mr. Mortimer then stood, hoping with his mitigation speech to get Dad a lighter sentence.

## THE SENTENCING

Mr. Mortimer went on and on about Dad's health and how he had suffered several heart attacks; also he was in receipt of character witness letters. This I found amusing, as where were these witnesses during the trial?

Right to the last he pleaded not guilty, and Mr. Mortimer continued with, "although found guilty, my client was a changed man."

The way he was talking, he made my dad out to be a model citizen.

The judge was getting visibly bored with his speech.

Again Mr. Mortimer went on: "my client has adapted well to prison life and is teaching inmates to read and write."

All sorts of images of him in prison flashed through my head; are these people abusers too?

He's priming them for the Internet, ready to groom young kids. I wouldn't put it past him.

This time the judge had his elbow on the desk and his chin and cheek in one hand.

"My client has been visited by his eldest son in prison."

I could feel Sarah's anger over this; I knew this would happen.

Then Mr. Mortimer slapped us all in the face by saying, "well, things couldn't have been that bad," or as bad as we had made out.

David went to stand, this statement had made him so angry; the judge was also unhappy at this remark. Both Sarah and I struggled to pin him back to his seat.

What a stab in the back for us, after Dad had been found guilty.

The tears began to flow from my eyes once more, but I still didn't take my eyes off the judge.

And still Mr. Mortimer went on about Dad's medication and how this must be taken into account.

The judge had heard enough and finally stopped him.

"Tell this to the prison service."

Once again, the judge spoke to Mr. Taylor and asked to clarify more legal points, then paused.

He looked to the middle of the room where Dad was in the dock.

This is it. Here we go, David, here we go, what we have been waiting for.

The judge boomed, "Would the defendant please rise. Can you hear me?"

A faint voice answered,

"Yes, Your Honour."

Then he continued,

## THE SENTENCING

"These offenses are dreadful offenses, and from what I have heard and seen, have blighted these children's lives considerably.

"You pleaded not guilty to these terrible crimes and yet you were found guilty, making your children suffer even further by having to give such harrowing accounts of their childhood. This is pure cowardice.

"I do believe even at your age you would still pose a threat to society, so therefore I am sentencing you to and on the count of rape and gross indecency. Ten years."

I welled up and tried hard to stay composed.

David was still shaking and mumbling.

Ten years, oh my God.

"The sentencing for the second daughter, Sarah, a sentence of two years, then eighteen months. For David, two years.

"That concludes the sentencing.

"I will permit that two years be taken into consideration for your age.

"Had you been a younger man, I would have no hesitation at sentencing you to life in prison.

"Take him down."

"Take him down, take him down," David repeated.

I did not turn to see those final moments.

We all cried and cried.

Altogether Dad received fourteen years; it was more than we ever expected.

"What a result, what a result," said David, still sobbing.

Uncle Phil only got five years, but he did plead guilty.

Mr. Taylor joined us outside the courtroom.

"I want to thank you for everything you have done for us, it's been a tough journey, but we all survived and now will only get stronger."

He continued to say that Mr. Mortimer told Dad to bring his suitcase with him today.

Dad would never walk the streets of this town again, and more likely die in prison.

Will I grieve for him? No.

I grieve only for my dead childhood, killed by him and Mother.

Mr. Taylor offered to take us all for a drink to celebrate. Wow, I did feel important that day. For the first time in my life, I felt like a real person.

## THE SENTENCING

The girls couldn't wait to get back to the station to celebrate. Dee and Hillery went back to the office to tell everyone the news.

We all ended up in a pub around the corner from the court, and Mr. Taylor insisted on treating us.

We chatted for about an hour, the events of the morning still buzzing through my head.

This book I have named *Behind Bars*.

I have spent forty years of my life behind bars imprisoned by my own shame, guilt, depression, and despair.

Now that caged door is open and I'm finally free.

We have swapped places, Dad and me, and now the bars are his—the bars he will be behind for the rest of his life.

I'm now free to step outside and live my life like never before.

No longer afraid to sleep at night, no longer shielding or hiding the way I feel.

This is me and I'm living it.

Mum too will not escape from her own prison.

She can remember and does remember, and it will stay with her.

I hope her guilt eats her away.

## BEHIND BARS

The magazine article named and shamed her too.

Now living in a nursing home, every day she will face her past.

Every day she will be alone. No one will visit, no family or friends.

Sarah was tugging at something around her neck as we left the pub.

"There is something I must do and it would be nice if we did it together."

She was wearing a crystal necklace that belonged to Mum.

She took it off; we all held it as she flung it into the nearby river.

The truth will set you free. This could not be more true for all of us—we told the truth and were believed, we have our closure; however my eldest brother Edward will still live in limbo, not truly living his life.

Dad bought his silence by ploughing money into his business.

He did not support us by telling the truth, and worst of all was not true to himself.

He will carry his burden of shame now to his grave. I can only hope before then he will find the strength to unload his own guilt, shame, depression, and tell someone the truth about his childhood.

Only then will he be truly free.

CHAPTER **24**

# The Ripple Effect

"Please get the phone, okay?" I could tell he was irritated by the constant ringing too. After all, it was interrupting his very important computer game.

I can hear muffled talking, then he put down the phone.

Returning to his room, I called out, "Well who was it?"

"Someone called Dee, she said can you call her back?" "Okay ta," I replied.

As I made my way down the stairs, the phone rang again.

"Hello, it's me." "Hi, Sarah." "I have had a call from Hillery and I'm sure Dee will contact you soon."

"I was just about to give her a call, what is it?"

"Well Hillery was going on about government cuts and how Next Link, the counseling service, is earmarked for closure, as they are funded by the police and there will be serious cuts in the budget.

"Well to cut to the chase, they will not get any funding next year and the service will close."

"Oh no," I replied, "that's terrible, they do such a fantastic job, without them I couldn't have coped with what we had to go through."

"Me neither," she replied.

The police and Next Link are asking for our help, all three of us."

"How?"

"They want us to go to the police headquarters and make a short film about what we have been through and the role of Next Link, and how important we think their help is.

"What do you think?"

"I would love to do it but I won't if you and David are against it."

"I think we need to support them and help if we can to secure their funding for the valuable work they do."

David also agreed after Sarah had spoken to him.

Arrangements were made for the three of us to spend the day at the police headquarters, where lunch would be provided and also transport to and from.

None of us knew what to expect; the girls also gave up their free time to help with the making of a short film. When completed, it will go to the home office and the funding bureaucrats to assist the application to be funded for the following year.

The police headquarters had their own filming studio.

We were all interviewed one by one; this did take up most of the day.

David, up until this point, had not received any counseling; when he was interviewed, the difference between us was so noticeable.

Still very angry at Mum and Dad, the depression and stress so visible on his face.

Outside of the courtroom on the day of the sentencing, a cameraman and reporter filmed us going into the court; we were stopped in our tracks as a prison van turned into the courtyard.

As the camera still rolled, it captured our worried faces.

Dad was in the back of that van.

When we left the courthouse, the filming started again, the relief on our faces captured on camera.

This truly was a moment that needed to be captured forever.

The short film was added to the film at the police centre and turned into a DVD named *The Ripple Effect*. The DVD was also used to help victims of abuse to realise they are not alone, they can talk, they will not be judged or ridiculed.

## BEHIND BARS

I truly hope our short film will help other victims of abuse to come to terms.

To get a step closer to the closure they deserve.

The ripple effect talks about how whole generations are affected by abuse; I know this to be true from my own family.

My boys, although I love them and cherish them, they too are victims of my abuse.

Missing out on a truly loving mum, I didn't fling my arms around them and tell them I loved them as much as I should have.

I have to live with that; my strong shell kept them out too.

"Your father and mother's actions have affected your children as well." These words from my counsellor were so true.

They did these things and made you feel inadequate as a mother and a wife.

You are not.

This is how the ripple effect is.

I'm sure I would have been a different person had I been allowed to find out about intimacy on my own instead of the way it was imposed on me in such a horrific way.

Since the closure Tom and I, well, we have learned so much about each other.

# THE RIPPLE EFFECT

We have talked and talked, everything now makes sense.

Although still learning lots about each other, I'm sure we have now put solid building blocks in place for our future.

We carry on learning more each time. This is a new beginning for us.

I'm very fortunate to get the chance to be truly happy and content with my life.

I finally feel free.

One day Mum and Dad will have to meet their maker and face their evil past.

My sons, when a bit older, also have the opportunity to truly understand and maybe forgive some of my ways.

I don't intend to spend any more of my time dwelling on the past; the past is done.

There is only room to move forward; the back door is now closed forever, and good riddance to it.

One day Sarah and David may decide to put pen to paper and tell their own story.

I will be there for them and encourage them every step of the way.

Their story is equally as horrific as my own.

◄ BEHIND BARS

We cried together outside the courtroom, truly united as brother and sisters.

The powerful message we sent out to the world.

Don't put up with abuse; it is a crime, a very serious crime.

My father thought he was untouchable, that he could walk between the raindrops.

We gave hope to many people by bringing this case to court.

I thank God we did.

The press coverage of our case brought with it many well-wishers and reading between the lines, messages from many people also affected by horrific and historic abuse. It was as if I could get inside their heads and see everything they were thinking.

Some of the comments from the press coverage speak for themselves.

I was so very moved.

*I would like to commend the both of you and your brother for your bravery in bringing this to the public attention and for sharing your experiences.*

*I and I suspect many others would secretly like to say a very big thank you to all three, for their courage, bravery, and generosity for making their private lives so public in order to help others who have been abused to come forward*

# THE RIPPLE EFFECT

*and make their abuser face justice, thus allowing them the chance to move on with their lives.*

*I myself went through similar things growing up, not as bad as you three had experienced but awful enough to leave an enormous impact on my life. I'm beginning to discover more and more people that have experienced similar situations and it does make me very angry to discover this.*

*I didn't consider myself a victim at the time, only when looking back, when I had grown up, and even though I am much younger than yourselves, was still not making use of the supposed system in place and contacts such as Childline.*

*It is such a delicate subject and difficult to detect, and I have heard that it is not unusual for family members to turn a blind eye, which is what happened in my case.*

*I would encourage anyone who has been through similar experiences to bring their stories to light as well.*

*These experiences create so much damage, and even though revealing them may not bring sufficient justice for the crime, at least it will show that it is no longer something that will be feared to speak about or brushed under the carpet.*

Also in the post, I received a letter from a neighbour; reading it brought tears to my eyes. Our story clearly touched the hearts of many people.

## BEHIND BARS

*13.12.2010*

*Dear Elizabeth, just a few lines to say, I saw your article in the Weekly Times and admire you, your brother, and your sister for speaking out. Katey remembers our speaking about this before but I don't know if I mentioned that I was abused as a child. Interestingly, I was at the age that you are now when I first started talking about it. It takes a long time to acknowledge the abuse; it is also the most difficult thing for abused people to admit. I didn't suffer as much as you did, but it was enough to leave me a bewildered person for many years. My older brother was driven to murder and suicide so I suppose I got off lightly. You may have discovered how useful writing can be in discharging old damage. I'm starting now to write about my past and it's an interesting process. I do hope you and your family have a good Christmas than the Christmases of past years.*

*With love.*
*Sally*

CHAPTER **25**

# Survivor

I often asked myself, am I really a survivor also?—asking myself how this wonderful transformation in me happened and still keeps on happening, discovering even more every day.

I now am familiar with the recovery process, and for me life just gets better and better. My hope is that after reading my story, people will have a better understanding of the process of recovery. There is a lot of shame attached to each memory of abuse that has to be worked through with careful and professional counseling. People often ask me, why did I not speak out sooner? These are people who do not understand the complete control that an abuser holds over his or her victim.

The process for a survivor starts with grieving; a person who loses a loved one would rarely be condemned for going through the stages of grief. It seems very different, however, for a survivor as well as those who love them to allow that same freedom and time to heal. Survivors have lost their childhood, their innocence, and their sense of value; many have lost the father or mother relationship so needed by children. In my case it was both of them. I did not have the skills or the tools to know how to work through these issues without help.

It took many years to get messed up inside and it may take many years to try and repair the damage and to heal, but there is hope and I would have to say we do get on with our lives; in fact, those of us in recovery are getting on with our lives, every day we hang in there. We may look pretty bad for a while, but so do people going through any other grieving process. The end result is absolutely worth it. The time has come for me now where there are no more nightmares or haunting memories to sort through. I am now ready to face life boldly and confidently because I have faced the ugly demons of the past and won! I needed that space and time to heal away from my husband too.

This space I found such a relief. Tom also has benefited from the space, evaluating his own issues and the realisation of the problems in our relationship and how everything began to slot into place.

Over the months that followed the case, we began to learn so much about one another. We talked openly and comfortably; it felt so right. This has only strengthened our relationship, and now my life has moved on in leaps and bounds. I look forward now to every new day and the challenges I can now handle with confidence. I never dreamt I would feel this way; miracles do happen, life is so good now. I consider myself a very lucky lady to have survived and moved on. I feel whole again because there are people who care. I feel strong because I have got through something awful. I have taken back control of my life and it feels so amazing.

CHAPTER **26**

# Tom and I

"I bullied you into marriage; in fact, I know now that I bullied you for a long time. I've been so stupid," said Tom.

"Do you think we could maybe go away for the weekend, and talk. I have so much still left in me that I want to say." He was so right; we both had been pulling our separate ways. We'd shut each other out.

I couldn't help thinking, how many other couples have suffered and how many relationships could be saved by releasing the absolute truth to one another?

We both went through a process of grieving for the lost years, the years of misunderstanding and confusion.

The truth really did set Tom free too.

"We have had such a rocky road, but now it feels as if we are on smoother ground.

"Please give me a chance."

## TOM AND I

Every time he spoke it was honest and heartfelt.

At the court Tom confided in Dee, and she explained to him that our relationship had been heavily strained because of the abuse I had suffered.

Tom was very upset and totally ashamed, even stating, "I have said and done some terrible things, I wish I could take all of it back.

"I want to give back the lost years, nothing to me is more important than trying to repair the damage I too have inflicted."

Dee went on to explain, "Your marriage was affected and was bound to have been a struggle.

"Victims of abuse rarely have happy relationships.

"This will undoubtedly have been the cause of all your frustration.

"I'm not saying that you dealt with it the right way, but lashing out was the only way for you at the time.

"Again you both married so young.

"For Elizabeth it was a way to escape, and the first person that she clung to was you."

She was so right.

We packed our little weekend bags; I'd managed to juggle my shifts at work to secure the weekend off. Looking forward so much to it. I didn't have a clue as to where we were going—he wanted to surprise me.

The hotel in Cornwall looked so lovely from the outside as we stopped the car in the marked bay.

This was my first visit to Fowey; the view from our room, and overlooking the bay, was breathtaking.

After sorting out the bags, we took a walk around the grounds, holding hands. It did feel so right.

Then in the evening we sat down to a wonderful meal together. Tom seemed a little bit anxious about something; I thought it best not to ask.

Again we took a stroll around the grounds and then went up to our room.

Tom closed the door and took both my hands; he had tears in his eyes.

"There is something I want to ask you," he said. "I will fully understand if you say no, but hear me out first, please.

"All of this and everything we have been through has been one hell of a journey, we have both learned so much about ourselves. I want to ask you if we can start again. A new start, a fresh beginning.

"What I'm trying to say is…"

He got down on one knee.

"Will you marry me again?"

A true tenderness and pure love was released on that night, as if it had been caged for years too.

I said, "YES."

Tom couldn't wait to get home and tell the boys, he was so excited. "I will book the church," he said, "and leave it all to me. "I don't want you getting stressed about anything. I am going to give you a most wonderful day that you will never forget, and also I have been working on something extra special." I was curious. "What is it?" "You will just have to wait and see."

As a little girl, I knew the sort of dress I wanted when I got married—the same sort of dress I chose for renewing my vows. A beautiful soft ivory flowing dress with a long veil. The colours for the maids of honour would be burgundy and ivory, and the cake the same with ribbons that had our names on them.

My boys all looked stunning in their suits and I did feel so proud.

Even the vicar hugged us after the ceremony, as she was well aware of our reasons for wanting this wonderful church service.

Then off to the reception. Everyone had a wonderful time and the celebrations carried on all weekend.

BEHIND BARS

Even now my workmates say what a fabulous time they all had.

My sister-in-law said she had never seen such an amazing spread, so much food.

Then the music came to a stop.

Tom had a piece of paper in his hand as he went for the microphone.

"I have written this little song for my darling wife. It has a very catchy verse so please feel free to join in."

He cleared his throat.

The song reduced everyone to tears, including me. I sat on a stool about four yards away as he sang this song to me.

I would dearly love to share it with you, but he wants to record it properly and has made arrangements to do just that.

The song sums up our lives and our struggles and the change after the court case was over. Our new beginning and our hope for the future.

When he finished, I jumped off my stool and planted a long kiss firmly on his lips, and we hugged each other so tight.

"I have one more surprise," he said. "Oh, what?" "Well you'd better start packing because on Friday we are off to Florida."

Really, I could not contain my excitement and skipped around the kitchen. "Yes, but that isn't all, we are going to sail on the FREEDOM OF THE SEAS and cruise around the Caribbean stopping off at Haiti, Jamaica, Mexico, St. Thomas, St. Maarten, Grand Cayman, and just one little itsy-bitsy private island, CocoCay . Unbelievable—all I'd dreamed of and more. Paradise, here we come.

My first cruise, and wow what a starter.

We had such an amazing time. I got to swim with dolphins and enjoy the onboard entertainment; there was just so much to do.

Best of all, it was both of us as husband and wife. Life just keeps getting better.